All-Occasion
Paper Crafting™

Edited by Vicki Blizzard

HOUSE
WHITE
BIRCH
PUBLISHER
SINCE 1947

All-Occasion Paper Crafting™

EDITOR	Vicki Blizzard
ART DIRECTOR	Brad Snow
PUBLISHING SERVICES MANAGER	Brenda Gallmeyer
ASSOCIATE EDITORS	Tanya Fox
ASSISTANT ART DIRECTOR	Nick Pierce
COPY SUPERVISOR	Michelle Beck
COPY EDITORS	Nicki Lehman, Mary O'Donnell, Beverly Richardson
TECHNICAL EDITOR	Läna Schurb
PHOTOGRAPHY	Tammy Christian, Don Clark, Christena Green, Matthew Owen
STYLISTS	Tammy Nussbaum, Tammy M. Smith
GRAPHIC ARTS SUPERVISOR	Ronda Bechinski
GRAPHIC ARTIST	Erin Augsburger, Pam Gregory
PRODUCTION ASSISTANTS	Cheryl Kempf, Marj Morgan
TECHNICAL ARTIST	Nicole Gage
CHIEF EXECUTIVE OFFICER	John Robinson
PUBLISHING DIRECTOR	David J. McKee
MARKETING DIRECTOR	Dan Fink
EDITORIAL DIRECTOR	Vivian Rothe

Printed in China
First Printing: 2005
Library of Congress Number: 2005924127
Hard Cover ISBN: 1-59217-086-2
Soft Cover ISBN: 1-59217-088-9

1 2 3 4 5 6 7 8 9

From the Editor

Don't you just love the holidays? I sure do, and I love creating fun projects using one of my favorite crafting media—paper!

Paper is so versatile, and there are just so many types for projects of all kinds. There's handmade paper with deep, rich textures. Mulberry paper is full of luscious threads and fibers. Vellum adds transparent beauty and elegance. Velvet paper resembles plush fabric. This book features all of these papers and more!

These projects are trendy and timely. Ornaments, home decor and altered art are featured prominently throughout, and while most of the designs are easily done by beginners, more experienced crafters also will be inspired by these projects.

We really enjoyed putting this book together, and we know you'll enjoy creating these unique projects for your home and for gifts.

Warm regards,

Vicki

CONTENTS

MEMORIES

REFLEC

CHEERS

2005

ETERN

New Year's Wishes

DESIGN BY SUSAN STRINGFELLOW

Send the gift of a glass charm along with good wishes for the New Year!

Project Note: Adhere pieces using glue stick unless instructed otherwise.

Score and fold 12 x 6-inch piece wheat card stock in half to form a 6-inch square card with fold at top. Rub edges of 5½-inch square of printed paper on ink pad; adhere printed paper to center of card.

Rub edges of a 1½ x 1-inch piece gold paper on ink pad; adhere in lower left quadrant of card. Use computer to generate, or hand-print, "Happy New Years!" on transparency to fit within gold paper; cut out and staple over gold paper. Rub a ½ x ¾-inch piece black paper with silver and gold metallic finishes. Adhere in lower left quadrant, overlapping gold paper. Punch two ⅛-inch holes down center; attach gold mini brads through holes.

Rub a 1¾ x 3¼-inch piece black paper with silver and gold metallic finishes. Adhere in upper right corner of card, ½ inch from edges. Punch ⅛-inch holes through front of card just outside upper corners of black paper; attach black mini brads through holes.

Create wine glass charm by threading sun/moon charm, and silver and gold beads onto wire ring. Lay atop handmade black paper on card. Thread metallic fiber through ring; wrap ends around black mini brads. Adhere sun/moon charm to black paper using adhesive dot.

Using rubber stamps and ink pad, randomly stamp surface of card with words—"Cheers," "Memories," "Reflect," "Eternity"—and year. ■

SOURCES: Printed paper from Mustard Moon; transparency from 3M; rubber stamps from Leave Memories; metallic rub-on finishes from Craf-T Products; wine charm ring from Hirschberg Schutz & Co. Inc.; sun/moon charm from Blue Moon Beads.

MATERIALS

Wheat card stock
Numerals printed paper
Black handmade paper
Gold textured paper
Printable transparency
Rubber stamps: alphabet, words, numerals
Black ink pad
Rub-on metallic finish: silver, gold
Mini brads: 2 gold, 2 black
Silver wire ring for wine-glass charm
Beads: gold, silver
Sun/moon charm
Metallic fiber
⅛-inch circle punch
Stapler and staplers
Glue stick
Adhesive dot
Computer (optional)
Computer font (optional)

Tiled Frame

DESIGN BY MARY AYRES

Paper glaze and tiles transform a basic wooden frame into an attractive home accent perfectly suited to display holiday greetings or photos.

MATERIALS
9 x 7-inch flat wooden frame
Printed papers with
   "texture" patterns (see
   Project Note)
Metallic gold paint
Texturizing medium
Paper glaze
Fine-grit sandpaper
Bristle paintbrush
Sponge
Paper glue
Computer (optional)
Computer fonts (optional)

Project Note: *Sample uses 11 different papers for tiles and a 12th for "Happy New Year" panel.*

Lightly sand frame; using paintbrush, paint all surfaces with one coat gold paint. Mix equal parts gold paint and texturizing medium; using sponge, dab mixture onto front and sides of frame to give it a textured appearance.

Cut 50–60 (¾-inch) squares from assorted papers. Lay them out on frame, leaving space between them and positioning them at slight angles. Use paper glue to adhere squares to frame. Using paintbrush, apply a single heavy coat of paper glaze over each square. Let dry overnight.

Use computer to generate, or hand-print, "Happy New Year" on printed paper so that words will fit in frame opening; use a different font for each letter. Trim lettered panel to fit in frame; mount in frame.

After the holiday, replace the "Happy New Year" panel with a favorite photo, if desired. ■

SOURCES: Texturizing medium from DecoArt; Aleene's Paper Glaze from Duncan.

Resolutions Note Board

DESIGN BY EILEEN HULL

Resolve to follow through with your New Year's resolutions! Posting them on an attractive note board will keep them fresh in your mind all year long.

Use computer to generate, or hand-print, New Year's resolutions on pale blue card stock to fit within rectangles no larger than 1½ x 1 inch; cut out. Adhere resolutions to cork using adhesive dots.

From pale blue mat board cut four ¾-inch squares and one piece 3¼ x 1 inches. Adhere mat board pieces to corrugated cardboard using double-sided adhesive tape. Trim around mat board, leaving 1/16-inch borders on squares and 1/8-inch borders on rectangle. Using paint pen, write numerals for year on mat board squares and "resolutions" on rectangle.

Punch 1/8-inch holes through upper corners of royal blue mat board, ¼ inch from edges. Set eyelets in holes. Thread ribbon through eyelets and knot for hanger.

Adhere year, "resolutions" and cork panel to royal blue mat board using double-sided adhesive tape. ■

SOURCE: Paint pen from Sakura.

MATERIALS

Mat board: 4½ x 7-inch royal blue, 4 x 2-inch pale blue
Pale blue card stock
Mini-corrugated cardboard
4-inch-square cork panel
2 light blue eyelets and eyelet-setting tool
5/8-inch-wide sheer metallic copper ribbon
Gold paint pen
Craft knife
1/8-inch hole punch
Clear adhesive dots
Double-sided adhesive tape
Computer (optional)
Computer font (optional)

Countdown to the Future

DESIGN BY SUSAN HUBER

Artist canvas provides an ideal surface for creating a unique New Year's gift. Open the book to reveal festive surprises and good wishes for the coming year!

MATERIALS

- 2 (6-inch-square) artist's canvases
- Black-and-white printed papers, including one with numerals
- Card stock: black, white
- 3½-inch-square slide mounts: black type on white, white type on black
- Rubber stamps: party tag, champagne bottle
- Black pigment ink pad
- Black chalk
- Black epoxy number and letter stickers
- Epoxy letter "bubble" stickers
- Silver star cutout
- Alphabet rub-on transfers
- Pewter buckle
- Pewter door knocker accent
- Black mini brads
- Eyelets: 4 black squares, 4 white stars
- ¾-inch-wide black twill tape with grommets
- Black-and-white narrow ribbons
- Fine black string or cord
- 2 (¾-inch) silver hinges with screws
- Circle punches: ⅛-inch, 1/16-inch
- Eyelet-setting tool
- Craft knife
- Screwdriver
- Paper glue
- Double-sided tape
- Craft adhesive
- Adhesive foam tape

FRONT COVER

Cut black card stock to cover front of one canvas; adhere using paper glue. Cut printed paper ¼ inch smaller; center and adhere to black card stock using paper glue.

Cut four 1⅛ x 2⅜-inch rectangles from numerals printed paper; adhere to black card stock and trim, leaving narrow black borders. Punch ⅛-inch hole in end of each rectangle; set black square eyelets in holes. Set white star eyelets in black square eyelets using eyelet-setting tool.

Using narrow ribbon, tie each tag through a grommet in a 7-inch piece of twill tape with grommets. Adhere twill tape across top of canvas using double-sided tape. Punch 1/16-inch hole in bottom edge of second tag from left; tie silver star cutout to tag using fine black string. Adhere black epoxy number stickers for "2006" to tags.

Cover sides of canvas with white-on-black 13/16-inch ribbon using double-sided tape.

INNER LEFT-HAND PAGE

Cut black card stock to cover back of artist canvas used for front cover; cut printed paper ¼ inch smaller; center and adhere to black card stock. Using craft knife, cut 2¾-inch-square window from center of paper/card-stock panel. Adhere panel to canvas using craft adhesive.

Cut 3 x 2½-inch rectangle from printed paper; adhere to black card stock and trim, leaving narrow black borders. Fold accordion-style into four panels. Adhere black epoxy number stickers for "2005" to accordion panels. Fit folded panels in opening. Adhere white-on-black slide mount over opening using double-sided tape.

Stamp party tag and champagne bottle onto white card stock using black ink pad; cut out and adhere to black card stock. Cut out, leaving narrow black border. Punch ⅛-inch hole in top of each; poke tips of black mini brads through strands of ribbon; attach mini brads through holes. Adhere tags in bottom corners using adhesive foam tape.

Make 2½ x ⅞-inch tag of white card stock matted on black. Punch ⅛-inch hole in left end; thread ribbon through hole. Apply black epoxy letter bubble stickers to tag to spell "PAST"; adhere tag in upper right corner using adhesive foam tape.

INNER RIGHT-HAND PAGE

Turn second canvas wrong side up. Cut black card stock to cover back; cut printed paper ¼ inch smaller; center and adhere to black card stock. Using craft knife, cut 2¾-inch-square window from center of paper/card stock panel. Adhere panel to back of canvas using craft adhesive.

Remove transparency from black-on-white slide mount; adhere slide mount over opening

using double-sided tape. Apply rub-on transfer letters to spell "DESTINY" onto upper left corner of page.

Cover sides of canvas with ribbon using double-sided tape. Weave ribbon through buckle; adhere ribbon up right side of page using double-sided tape; wrap ribbon ends over edges and adhere on back of page (front of canvas). Adhere black epoxy letter bubble stickers to spell "FUTURE" in lower right corner.

For mini book, piece together black card stock to make a strip 1¾ x 21¼ inches; fold strip accordion-style nine times to make a total of 10 pages. Open strip and lay flat. On one side, adhere rectangle of printed paper cut ¼ inch smaller to each page. On other side, adhere a rectangle of another printed paper to each page except the page on the far left; adhere this page inside canvas window using double-sided tape.

On first side, count down to the new year by applying black epoxy number stickers to each page, beginning with 10, 9, 8, etc. On second side, apply black epoxy word stickers to read "Happy New Year." Fold pages to tuck book into opening in canvas. Adhere door knocker to the first page using craft adhesive.

BACK COVER & ASSEMBLY

Turn inner right-hand page over. Cut black card stock to cover canvas; adhere. Cut printed paper ¼ inch smaller; center and adhere to black card stock. Attach canvases with hinges. ■

SOURCES: Printed papers from Creative Imaginations and 7gypsies; ribbons and twill with grommets from Fibers By The Yard; epoxy letters from K&Company; epoxy stickers, numbers and letters, slide mounts and rub-on transfers from Creative Memories; metal star and buckle from Making Memories; rubber stamps from Magenta; door knocker from EK Success.

Moments to Remember

DESIGN BY SAM COUSINS

Never lose track of special occasions and dates to remember again! This perpetual calendar is a quick reference to keep and update from year to year.

MATERIALS

8-inch-square mini album
Printed papers
Card stock
Word, alphabet, quotation, number and picture stickers
Embellishments and images for inside pages
"Moments" bubble phrase
Clock face bookplate
Month rubber stamps
Distress ink
3/8- to 3/4-inch-wide ribbons
Black permanent fine-tip marker
Ruler
Instant-dry paper glue
Computer with calendar-making program (optional)

Cut printed paper to fit behind opening in album cover; adhere. Spell out title in center using alphabet stickers; outline stickers with black fine-tip marker if desired.

Cut 7¾-inch square of printed paper. Using opening in album cover as a guide, tear opening in paper so title will show through. Turn paper over; mark lines from inner corner to outer corner. Cut along lines to create four sections. Rub edges of sections with ink; adhere sections to album cover, separating sections slightly.

Tie ribbon around front cover next to spine. Knot assorted ribbons onto this ribbon.

Adhere quotation sticker across bottom of cover; adhere "moments" bubble phrase under clock face bookplate on right side.

CALENDAR TABS

Cut six 2-inch squares of printed paper; fold in half. Lay tabs with folds at top; stamp both sides with consecutive months, positioning words near folds of tabs—January and February on one tab, March and April on the next, etc.

Adhere tabs over edges of pages in order, staggering their positions down side of album.

CALENDAR PAGES

Use computer to generate a calendar grid measuring approximately 6 x 5¾ inches for each page. **Option:** *Use pattern provided to draw calendar grids.* Add numbers to blocks using rubber stamps, stickers or black fine-tip marker. Adhere each calendar grid to card stock; trim, leaving border.

Adhere a 7½ x 7⅝-inch piece of printed paper or card stock to each album page. Adhere matted calendar pages to album pages, positioning calendars toward bottom. Add month names using stickers or rubber stamps. Embellish pages as desired, matching embellishments to the months.

Add birthdays, anniversaries, etc., to calendar pages using black fine-tip marker. ■

SOURCES: Mini album from Bazzill; papers and embellishments from Die Cuts With A View; additional embellishments from Karen Foster Design, me and my BIG ideas, Doodlebug Design, EK Success, Pebbles Inc., Sticker Café and Sticker Studio; alphabet stickers from Karen Foster Design, me and my BIG ideas, Creative Imaginations, KI Memories, NRN Designs and Wordsworth; bubble phrase from Li'l Davis Designs; clock face bookplate from Karen Foster Design; rubber stamps from Magnetic Poetry.

PATTERN ON PAGE 158

very

IMPORTANT

dates

moments

January

July

March

May

it's not the years in your life that count
it's the life in your years

feBRuaRy

1	2	3	4	5	6	7
	Sarah's Birthday				Matt's B-day	
8	9	10	11	12	13	14
				Ben's B-day		Valentine's Day
15	16	17	18	19	20	21
Suz's B-day						
22	23	24	25	26	27	28

♥ hugs & kisses ♥

USA JULY

1	2	3	4	5	6
			4th of July		Ben's B-day
8	9	10	11	12	13	14
15	16	17	18	19	20	21
22	23	24	25	26	27
29	30	31

UNITED WE STAND

AUGUST

1	2	3	4	5	6	7
8	9	10	11	12	13	14
15	16	17	18	19	20	21
22	23	24	25	26	27	28
29	30	31

beach BUM

MATERIALS

5-inch plastic foam cube
Card stock: chartreuse, hot
    pink, purple
Rubber stamps: circle
    background, flowers
    ranging in size from
    ¾–3¾ inches, "Happy
    New Year"
Black pigment ink
Black embossing powder
Black craft paint
14-inch bamboo skewers
Wooden party picks
Embossing heat tool
Craft knife
Circle punches: 1-inch, 1¾-
    inch
Paper trimmer with scoring
    blade (optional)
Straight pins
Paintbrush
Craft scissors
½-inch-wide double-sided
    adhesive tape
Black adhesive foam squares
Paper glue

Floral Fantasy Party Set

DESIGNS BY LORINE MASON

Brightly colored papers and stamped images will add to the festive nature of your New Year's celebration.

LARGER FLOWERS

Using black pigment ink and flower stamps, stamp assorted flower images on chartreuse, pink and purple card stock. Sprinkle with black embossing powder; emboss.

Using craft knife, trim centers and sections from images to make flowers of different sizes. Trim around individual petals within some images and bend petals forward slightly for added dimension.

Using paper glue and/or adhesive foam squares, build flowers in layers.

SMALLER FLOWERS

Using 1¾-inch circle punch, punch circles from chartreuse, pink and purple card stock. Run edges over embossing ink pad; sprinkle with black embossing powder and emboss. Stamp flower images within circles; emboss. Add additional stamped, embossed layers as desired.

CENTERPIECE

Referring to Fig. 1, cut and score 8½ x 11-inch sheet chartreuse card stock, cutting along solid lines and scoring along dashed lines. Adhere ½-inch-wide double-sided tape to areas indicated by X's.

Referring to Fig. 2, trim two sheets purple card stock to 5 x 10 inches; score along dashed line. Adhere ½-inch-wide double-sided tape to areas indicated by X's.

Cover right side of cube with chartreuse card stock, tape side up, folding tabs over edges onto top, front and back. Secure card stock with straight pins. Repeat to cover left side.

Cover back and top of cube with purple card stock, tape side down, adhering purple card stock to chartreuse card stock and removing pins as you work. Repeat to cover front and top of cube with purple card stock, overlapping on top.

Following previous instructions, make four larger flowers and three smaller ones. Make also one flower approximately 2⅝ inches in diameter for front of cube. Punch seven 1-inch circles from card stock.

Paint seven bamboo skewers black. Sandwich blunt ends between 1-inch circle and large or small flower; adhere using paper glue.

Using black pigment ink, stamp "Happy New Year" twice onto pink card stock and circle background onto chartreuse card stock; sprinkle with black embossing powder and emboss.

Trim "Happy New Year" rectangles to 4½ x 1⅜ inches. Cut 5½ x 3⅞-inch rectangle from purple card stock and a 3-inch square from chartreuse. Run edges of all rectangles and squares over black pigment ink pad; sprinkle with black embossing powder and emboss.

Using a craft knife, cut center rectangle out of embossed chartreuse circle background panel, leaving a "window." Using paper glue, center and adhere circle panel to purple rectangle. Using adhesive foam squares, adhere one pink "Happy New Year" rectangle at an angle over chartreuse/purple panel. Adhere completed panel to skewer below a large flower.

Using paper glue, adhere 3-inch chartreuse square at an angle to front of cube; using adhesive foam squares, adhere pink "Happy New Year" rectangle and 2⅝-inch flower over chartreuse square.

Using craft scissors, cut skewers on flowers to desired heights. Insert skewers into top of cube.

PARTY PICKS

Following instructions for smaller flowers, make small flowers from card stock. Sandwich end of each wooden party pick between a flower and a 1-inch circle punched from card stock; adhere using paper glue.

Use as skewers for party snacks.

CONTINUED ON PAGE 158

Celebration Favors

DESIGNS BY KATHY WEGNER

Personalized paper hats with party blow-outs and glass charms add to the festivities of any occasion.

PAPER HATS

Project Note: *Adhere pieces using craft glue unless otherwise indicated.*

For each favor, wrap mulberry paper around snow-cone cup; adhere using double-sided adhesive tape. Fold excess paper over rim; adhere inside cup. Wrap two strands of sparkle yarn around cup near rim; adhere.

Tassel: Wrap sparkle yarn around three fingertips four times; tie in center with another piece of yarn. Clip loops and fluff to form tassel. Cut point off hat; adhere knot of tassel in top of hat.

Thread tag onto sparkle yarn; tie yarn in a bow. Tie double strand of sparkle yarn around blow-out in a bow. Secure bows with dots of glue.

Apply glue to back of blow-out; let it set for a few moments until thickened. Press blow-out onto side of hat; let dry flat. Personalize tag; adhere to hat next to blow-out. ■

SOURCE: Kid's Choice! Glue from Beacon.

MATERIALS
Paper snow-cone cups
Mulberry papers *or* other
    handmade papers
1½ x 1-inch white card
    stock tags
Paper party blow-outs
Iridescent white sparkle fiber
¼-inch-wide double-sided
    adhesive tape
Craft glue

GLASS CHARMS

For each charm, thread wire ring almost full with 27–33 clear and colored beads. Bend ends of rings and pinch using needle-nose pliers.

Adhere adhesive sheet to mulberry paper, choosing paper color to match colored beads. Adhere mulberry paper to both sides of card stock tag; trim off excess. Punch ¹⁄₁₆-inch hole through hole in tag.

Tie tag onto center of charm with a bow of sparkle yarn; secure knot with craft glue. Personalize tag if desired. ■

SOURCE: Kid's Choice! Glue from Beacon.

MATERIALS
Mulberry papers *or* other
    handmade papers
1½ x 1-inch white card
    stock tags
Silver wire rings for wine-
    glass charms
Glass E-beads: clear
    iridescent, plus colors to
    match mulberry papers
Iridescent white sparkle fiber
¹⁄₁₆-inch circle punch
Needle-nose pliers
Adhesive sheet
Craft glue

New Year's Eve Memories

DESIGN BY SUSAN STRINGFELLOW

The unique shape of this book makes it ideal for commemorating New Year's Eve celebrations.

COVERS

Take book apart. Trace around covers onto green printed card stock; cut out. Cut two bottle shapes from another paper for inside covers. Adhere papers to covers with double-sided tape. Rub edges with black solvent ink pad; repunch holes with ⅛-inch circle punch.

Cut 3¼ x 2½-inch rectangle from gold printed card stock for bottle label; rub edges with black solvent ink pad. Adhere label to cover using double-sided tape. Repunch holes.

Stamp grapes on front cover in upper left and lower right; color with watercolor pencils and paintbrush.

Spell "memories" up left edge of cover using alphabet stickers. Use computer to generate, or hand-print, "New Year's Eve" *reversed* on burgundy card stock; cut out letters with craft knife and adhere to cover with paper glaze. Stamp "Festivities" onto label just below "New Year's Eve" with black solvent ink pad.

Following manufacturer's directions, rub gold leaf onto top 1½ inches of bottle neck, including edges. Seal both covers with two coats decoupage medium.

Stamp "Our Family" on round printed card-stock tag with black solvent ink pad; rub edges with ink pad. Seal tag with two coats decoupage medium. Punch ¼-inch hole in tag; tie tag and grapes charm around neck of bottle with ribbon.

PAGES

Cover backgrounds of pages with printed card stock; adhere with double-sided tape. Layer photos on printed papers as desired; adhere to pages with double-sided tape. Embellish with fibers, trims, stickers, tags, fasteners, tabs, eyelets, etc., adhering them with paper glaze.

Cut additional smaller pages from printed paper or card stock; adhere photos with double-sided tape and embellish as desired. Punch holes along edge to fit spiral binding; insert them between bottle-shaped pages when reassembling book. ∎

SOURCES: Scrapbook from The Little Scrapbook Store; card stock and tag from Basic Grey; sparkle card stock from Prism; rubber stamps from Stampin' Up! and RubberStamp Ave.; solvent ink pad from Tsukineko Inc.; charm from Create-A-Craft; gold leaf from Mona Lisa Products; decoupage medium from Plaid.

MATERIALS

Spiral-bound wine-bottle scrapbook
Printed card stocks: bottle green, gold, and matching 1¾-inch circle tag
Assorted printed papers
Burgundy sparkle card stock
Alphabet stickers
Rubber stamps: grapes and words
Black solvent ink pad
Silver grapes charm
12 inches ⅝-inch-wide ribbon
Additional embellishments as desired
Rub-on gold leaf
Watercolor pencils
Decoupage medium
Small paintbrush
Circle punches: ⅛-inch, ¼-inch
Craft knife
Paper piercer or awl
Double-sided tape
Decoupage medium
Paper glaze
Computer (optional)
Computer font (optional)

True Love

DESIGN BY MARY AYRES

Computer-generated vintage rose images and letters give a truly romantic look to this frame.

Sand frame lightly. Using bristle paintbrush, paint front and sides brown; using foam brush, brush painted surfaces with crackle medium. Let dry. Using bristle paintbrush, paint all surfaces of frame with one coat cream paint; cracks will appear.

Print rose images onto photo paper. **Option:** *Use stickers or images from magazines or greeting cards.* Cut out. Brush backs of images with jewel glue; adhere roses to front of frame, folding images over onto sides. Overlap some images leaving some crackled finish showing. Trim excess paper.

Using bristle brush, dry-brush frame edges with metallic gold paint. Using large foam brush, brush one coat laminating liquid over front and sides of frame. When dry, rub fingers over frame wherever paper is starting to come up.

Wrap ribbon around upper left and lower right corners of frame; using permanent adhesive, adhere ends on back.

Use computer to generate, or hand-print, letters for "TRUE LOVE" using a different font and a different color card stock for each letter. Cut out letters centered in circles that will fit on top of bottle caps. Using permanent adhesive, adhere letters to bottle caps.

Sand edges of letter circles even with bottle caps. Using sponge, rub edges of circles with metallic gold ink. Using adhesive foam squares, adhere bottle caps to ribbons. ■

SOURCES: Frame from Structural Industries; Sweet Roses CD-ROM from The Vintage Workshop; acrylic paint and crackle medium from DecoArt; Fabri-Tac permanent adhesive, Gem-Tac jewel glue and Liquid Laminate from Beacon.

MATERIALS

- 8 x 10-inch flat wooden easel frame
- Card stock: small pieces in 8 shades of pink and red
- Flat-finish photo paper (optional)
- Rose images on CD-ROM (optional)
- Metallic gold ink pad
- Acrylic paints: brown, cream, metallic gold
- Crackle medium
- Laminating liquid
- 8 bottle caps
- ½-inch-wide olive green ribbon
- Fine-grit sandpaper
- Small piece of sponge
- Bristle paintbrush
- Foam paintbrush
- ½-inch adhesive foam squares
- Jewel glue
- Permanent adhesive
- Computer
- Computer fonts (optional)

Love Sentiments

DESIGN BY SHERRY L. WRIGHT

Express your love with sweet messages tucked into the pocket of this altered CD.

MATERIALS

Blank CD
Printed and embossed
    papers
2½-inch-wide manila
    envelope
Craft paint in a coordinating
    color
Domed epoxy stickers
"E" alphabet ticket tag
Alphabet rub-on transfers:
    "I," "L," "V"
15/16-inch-square metal
    "U" stencil
Padlock and key charms
"O" brad
Ribbons
Rickrack and braid trims
Petals from white silk flower
Adhesive-backed magnet
    strips
Fine-grit sandpaper
Stapler and staples
Circle punch
Craft knife
Paintbrush
Decoupage medium

Project note: *Use decoupage medium as glue throughout.*

Sand CD so that decoupage medium will adhere. Trace around CD twice onto printed paper; cut out. Adhere paper to front of CD; set second circle aside.

Paint manila envelope; tear across open end to form 2½ x 3-inch pocket. Adhere printed paper over bottom half of pocket; punch hole in bottom right corner. Embellish pocket with strip of contrasting papers and braid trim. Cut strips from assorted paper to fit in pocket; write love notes on strips. Staple ribbon "tails" to one end of strips; tuck into pocket.

Arrange transfers, ticket tag, metal stencil and "O" brad on tag and pocket to spell "I LOVE U"; adhere, sticking "O" brad through silk flower petals. Thread ribbon through hole in pocket; tie metal "U" stencil near one end. Knot padlock and key charms onto opposite ends of ribbon.

Embellish CD as desired using motifs cut from embossed paper, braid, rickrack and domed epoxy stickers. Tie knot in center of ribbon for hanger; adhere ends to back of CD. Adhere remaining paper circle to back of CD; adhere magnet strips to back of CD. ■

SOURCES: Papers and domed epoxy stickers from K&Company; rub-on transfers from Making Memories and me & my BIG Ideas; ticket tag from Li'l Davis Designs; metal letter stencil from Scrapworks; lock-and-key charm from Darice.

Chocolate Treasures

DESIGN BY SUSAN STRINGFELLOW

Fill this tiny chest with candy kisses for your sweetheart as a token of your love this Valentine's Day!

Project Note: Use paper glaze as adhesive throughout.

Paint inside of box pink.

Cover bottom outside of box with striped paper; rub edges lightly with black ink pad. Use alphabet stamps to stamp "kisses" around box. Attach "be mine" license plate to front of box in lower right corner using silver mini brads. Poke cream mini brad through center of flower; attach just above license plate.

Cover box lid, including ends, with polka-dot paper; rub edges lightly with black ink pad. Tie pink and blue ribbons around lid, positioning pink bow at right edge and blue bow in center; secure with dots of paper glaze. String heart charm on brown sheer ribbon; knot onto pink ribbon on left side; notch ribbon ends.

Paint centers of hearts on "chocolates" license plate with paper glaze; sprinkle with pink ultrafine glitter. Attach license plate to lid using silver mini brads. Attach two flowers above license plate using cream mini brads. ∎

SOURCES: Papers and ribbons from SEI; rubber stamps from Hero Arts; license plates from Junkitz; charm from Darice; paper glaze from JudiKins.

MATERIALS
3½ x 3½ x 4-inch papier-
    mâché trunk box
Printed papers: stripes,
    polka-dots
Pink pearlescent paint
Alphabet rubber stamps
Black ink pad
License plates: "chocolates,"
    "be mine"
Mini brads: 4 silver; 3 cream
Silver heart charm
3 silk flowers
Ribbons: ³/₁₆-inch-wide pink
    and blue, ⁹/₁₆-inch-wide
    sheer brown
Pink ultrafine glitter
Paintbrush
Paper piercer *or* awl
Paper glaze

Hearts & Bows Trio

DESIGNS BY HELEN L. RAFSON

Embroidery floss stitched over corrugated cardboard hearts creates a simple yet sophisticated trio for Valentine's Day.

MATERIALS

- 3 x 6-inch cream pillar candle
- Slender 12-inch wooden dowel
- 5½ x 4-inch white note card
- Mauve corrugated paper
- Pink card stock
- Mauve acrylic paint
- 3 (1-inch) brass Cupid charms
- 3 (1-inch) mauve ribbon roses
- 13½ inches ⅛-inch-wide pink ribbon
- 6 (11-inch) pieces ¼-inch-wide pink ribbon
- 10 inches ⅝-inch-wide light pink ribbon
- 5½ inches pink baby rickrack
- Variegated mauve embroidery floss
- Pink sewing thread
- Tapestry needle
- Hand-sewing needle
- Paintbrush
- Seam sealant
- Craft glue
- Paper glue
- Instant-dry paper glue

Project Note: Use craft glue unless instructed otherwise.

HEART

Using pattern provided, cut heart from mauve corrugated paper so that ridges run vertically and one "valley" runs down center. Mark dots in each "valley" ⅛ inch from edge. Using tapestry needle, punch holes at dots.

Thread tapestry needle with variegated mauve floss; knot end. Starting on one side of heart, work straight stitches down valleys from hole to hole. Knot ends of floss; adhere knots on back.

Hold two pieces of ¼-inch-wide pink ribbon together; tie in a bow. Separate bow loops slightly. Trim ribbon ends at an angle; treat ends with seam sealant.

Sew Cupid charm to back of bow using hand-sewing needle and pink sewing thread. Adhere ribbon rose over bow knot. Adhere bow and charm to heart.

CANDLE

Make one heart as directed above.

Treat ends of ⅝-inch-wide light pink ribbon with seam sealant. Wrap ribbon around candle near bottom; overlap ends on back and adhere.

Using pattern provided, cut one heart from pink card stock. Trim slightly smaller than corrugated heart; adhere to back of corrugated heart using paper glue. Adhere heart to candle using instant-dry paper glue.

PLANT POKE

Make one heart as directed above.

Using pattern provided, cut one heart from pink card stock. Trim slightly smaller than corrugated heart; adhere to back of corrugated heart using paper glue.

Paint dowel with two coats mauve paint. Adhere end of ⅛-inch-wide pink ribbon at end of dowel using craft glue. Spiral ribbon around dowel. Adhere other end of ribbon to dowel using craft glue.

Adhere heart to end of dowel using craft glue.

NOTE CARD

Make one heart as directed above.

Position note card with fold at top. Adhere pink baby rickrack along bottom edge. Adhere heart to center of card. ■

SOURCES: Charms from Halcraft USA Inc.; Kid's Choice! Glue and Paper-Tac adhesive from Beacon.

PATTERNS ON PAGE 159

Princess Diary

DESIGN BY KATHY WEGNER

MATERIALS
Mini composition book
Pink bottle caps printed
   paper
Pink bottle caps stickers
2 blank bottle caps
5-inch (or longer) pink zipper
Pink fuzzy fiber
Hammer
Craft drill or small nail
Pink glitter glue
Double-sided adhesive sheet
Thick tacky glue
Clear adhesive strips
½-inch adhesive dots

Princesses old and young will cherish this tiny journal that's just right for recording wishes and dreams!

Adhere double-sided adhesive sheet to back of paper. Cut paper to fit front and back covers of composition book, avoiding spine. Adhere paper to covers.

Measure length of book spine for length of zipper needed; apply tacky glue across zipper where it will be cut. When dry, cut zipper and adhere adhesive strips to back of zipper; press zipper onto spine with zipper pull at top.

Lay bottle caps on protected work surface, edges down. Flatten bottle caps with hammer. Drill hole in edge of one bottle cap. Apply stickers to rounded sides of all bottle caps; on bottle cap with hole, apply another sticker to inside.

Tie pink fuzzy fiber through hole in zipper pull; tie other end through hole in bottle cap so that it dangles from bottom when book is closed over fiber.

Adhere remaining bottle caps to front of book using adhesive dots. Squeeze "splashes" of pink glitter glue onto cover, radiating out from bottle caps. Enhance stickers with pink glitter glue as desired. ■

SOURCE: Paper and stickers from Design Originals.

Valentine Romance

DESIGN BY LORINE MASON

Translucent vellum teamed with subtle rose-print paper gives a soft, romantic look to this napkin ring and votive duo.

CANDLE LAMP

Using pattern provided, cut lamp shade from printed paper and pink vellum. Trim ½ inch off bottom of paper lamp shade.

Lay vellum lamp shade over paper one, matching top edges. Fold pieces of tape in half lengthwise over side edges, securing layers. Using decorative-edge scissors, trim top edge of lamp shade. Reverse scissors; trim bottom edge.

Punch a ¹⁄₁₆-inch hole ³⁄₁₆ inch from left edge of lamp shade and ⅜ inch from bottom of vellum. Punch eight more holes up left edge, evenly spaced. Punch matching holes along right edge.

Beginning in bottom pair of holes, lace sides of lamp shade together with ¹⁄₁₆-inch-wide ribbon, crisscrossing ribbons as if tying a shoe. Knot ribbons at top.

Thread ⁵⁄₁₆-inch heart bead onto each ribbon tail; trim ribbon ends and knot. Using paper glue, adhere ³⁄₁₆-inch heart beads evenly along bottom of lamp shade.

Set votive candle in goblet; fit lamp shade over goblet.

NAPKIN RING

Cut 5 x 1¾-inch strip from printed paper and pink vellum. Trim off ½ inch along one long edge of paper strip.

Referring to instructions for lamp shade, secure side edges with tape; punch five holes up edges of strip and lace together using ¹⁄₁₆-inch-wide ribbon. Knot ⁵⁄₁₆-inch heart beads on ribbon ends.

Slide napkin ring over rolled-up napkin. ■

SOURCE: Paper-Tac paper glue from Beacon.

PATTERN ON PAGE 159

MATERIALS

Rose printed paper
Pink vellum
Glass candle goblet
Votive candle
Pink glass heart-shaped
   beads: approximately 18
   (³⁄₁₆-inch) *and* 4 (⁵⁄₁₆-inch)
Pink ¹⁄₁₆-inch-wide satin
   ribbon
¹⁄₁₆-inch circle punch
Decorative-edge scissors
Satin-finish transparent tape
Paper glue

Love Notes

DESIGN BY TAMI MAYBERRY

Passing love notes has never been more fun! Leave a special message for your valentine on this clipboard designed with love.

MATERIALS

Clipboard
Pen
Cork sheet *or* tile
4 x 1¾-inch laminate sample chip
6 x 4-inch white index cards *or* note cards
Aerosol primer
Acrylic paints: red, white
Crackle medium
"love" rubber stamp
Red ink pad
⅝-inch-wide "Love" ribbon: red, white
2½-inch foam alphabet stamps
Silver "love" charms
Red epoxy letter squares to spell "LOVE"
White alphabet rub-on transfers
Round red "Love" label
Paintbrushes
Foam brush
Craft cement
Clear or white silicone adhesive

Project Note: Adhere all pieces using craft cement unless instructed otherwise.

Cut cork to 8½ x 6¾ inches. Spray clipboard and cork with primer. Paint clipboard red. When dry, apply a thin coat of crackle medium using foam brush, following manufacturer's instructions. Apply a coat of white paint.

Paint cork with two coats white paint. Brush edges with red paint. Using red paint as ink, stamp "NOTES" across bottom of cork using foam alphabet stamps.

Paint rough side of laminate chip red. Adhere to left edge of clipboard 5 inches from bottom, allowing 1¼ inches of end with hole to protrude from edge.

Adhere cork to clipboard using silicone adhesive. Wrap white "Love" ribbon around cork panel; adhere ribbon ends on back of clipboard. Adhere red epoxy squares in upper left corner of clipboard; transfer white letters for "LOVE" to epoxy squares. Adhere round "Love" label on right side of clipboard, just above cork.

Knot five pieces of red "Love" ribbon onto left side of clipboard clip; repeat on right side. Using red ink pad and rubber stamp, stamp "love" in bottom right corner of index cards; secure cards under clipboard clip.

Thread charms onto accompanying chain; secure through hole in laminate chip. Clip pen onto laminate chip. ∎

SOURCES: Epoxy squares from Stickopotamus; alphabet rub-on transfers and "Love" label from Making Memories; rubber stamp from Village Arts Press.

Vintage Love

DESIGN BY MARY AYRES

Cherished love notes can be tucked safely away inside this treasure box adorned with lovely floral papers and brass embellishments.

MATERIALS

Wooden cigar box
5 different printed papers
Neutral parchment card
    stock
Gold ink pad
Acrylic paints: bright red,
    cool neutral, black
4 brass corners
4¼ x 2¾-inch brass frame
2¼ x 1⅛-inch brass
    bookplate
2 gold mini brads
Laminating liquid
1/16-inch circle punch
Fine-grit sandpaper
Pencil
Bristle paintbrush
Foam paintbrushes
Small sponge
Permanent adhesive
Jewel glue
Computer (optional)
Computer font (optional)

Remove labels from cigar box; sand box lightly. Using bristle paintbrush, paint exterior of cigar box with one coat red paint, avoiding hardware. Paint one coat cool neutral over red. Sand box lightly so that some red shows through.

Cut four rectangles of different sizes, one each from a different printed paper, to cover top of box and overlap in center. Using dry sponge, rub edges with gold ink. Brush backs of rectangles with jewel glue; adhere rectangles to box lid.

Using large foam brush, brush one coat laminating liquid over top of box. When dry, rub fingers over top of box wherever paper starts to come up.

Sand bookplate. Brush with black paint; wipe off excess. Use computer to generate, or hand-print, "LOVE" on remaining printed paper. Trim word to fit behind bookplate; using permanent adhesive, adhere rectangle to back of bookplate.

Cut a 4 x 2½-inch rectangle from parchment card stock; using dry sponge, rub edges with gold ink. Center bookplate in rectangle; using pencil, mark positions of bookplate holes on parchment. Punch ¹⁄₁₆-inch holes at marks. Attach bookplate to card stock using mini brads.

Using permanent adhesive, adhere card stock to center of box lid; adhere brass frame over edges of parchment rectangle; adhere brass corners to corners of box lid. ■

SOURCES: Printed papers from K&Company; brass frame and corners from Plaid; Gem-Tac jewel glue, Fabri-Tac permanent adhesive and Liquid Laminate from Beacon.

From the Heart

DESIGN BY LORETTA MATEIK

Micro beads and heart-themed ribbon grace the edges of this Valentine gift box filled with tokens of your affection.

Stamp "From the Heart" on white card stock using watermark ink pad; sprinkle with red embossing powder and emboss. Using box lid as a template, cut out stamped message, centering it in heart.

Run a 1 x 11-inch strip white card stock through paper crimper. Starting at top center of heart, adhere strip around box using double-sided tape, aligning edge of strip with bottom of box. Cut off any excess.

Adhere stamped heart to box lid using double-sided tape.

Wrap double-sided tape around top edge of lid so that about ⅛ inch is adhered to side and remaining tape protrudes evenly above top. Fold tape over onto top of lid, clipping as needed so tape lies flat. Peel off protective paper backing and cover tape with a mixture of red and clear micro beads.

Adhere ribbon around edges of lid using additional double-sided tape. Tie a small bow from a separate piece of ribbon; adhere to edge of lid at point. ■

SOURCES: Rubber stamp from Stampin' Up!; ink pad from Tsukineko Inc.

MATERIALS
Small papier-mâché box with lid
White card stock
"From the Heart" rubber stamp
Watermark ink pad
Red embossing powder
Micro beads: red, clear
³⁄₈-inch-wide hearts ribbon
Embossing heat tool
Paper crimper
½-inch-wide double-sided tape

Banner of Love

DESIGN BY SHERRY L. WRIGHT

Stencil letters grace the front of this beautiful wall hanging that doubles as a mini picture album.

MATERIALS

3 x 4-inch card-stock
    stencils: "L," "O,"
    "V," "E"
Printed and embossed
    papers
Textured card stock
Photos
Distress ink
White acrylic paint (optional)
Domed epoxy stickers
¾-inch 2-hole hinges
Wire clips: flower, heart
    and spiral
Heart brads
Petals from white silk flower
Satin and organza ribbons
Braid trims
Rickrack
Fine-grit sandpaper
    (optional)
Circle punch
Craft knife
Paintbrush (optional)
Glue stick
Craft glue

Project Note: Adhere pieces using glue stick unless instructed otherwise.

Adhere assorted printed and embossed papers to fronts of stencils. Trim out openings in letters using a craft knife.

Adhere contrasting printed and embossed papers to backs of stencils so that patterns show through openings. Adhere 3 x 4-inch pieces of textured card stock to backs of stencil panels.

Rub edges and raised areas of stencil panels with distress ink.

Punch holes in corners for connecting panels later: Punch holes in bottom corners only of "L" and top corners only of "E"; punch holes in all four corners of "O" and "V."

"L" and "V" panels will open like mini albums. Cut two 3 x 4-inch rectangles from textured card stock for back covers; attach one to each panel along edge using a hinge secured with two heart brads. *Option: First "distress" hinges and metal clips by painting them white; when dry, rub with fine-grit sandpaper.* Hold panels closed with wire clips.

Thread ribbons through holes to connect panels; knot ends on front. For hanger, adhere ends of a ribbon inside "L" panel using craft glue; tie coordinating ribbons at top of hanger. Completed banner will measure approximately 24 inches.

Embellish fronts of panels using epoxy stickers, ribbon, braid trims, rickrack, wire clips and petals from silk flowers; adhere using craft glue.

Turn hanging over. Adhere photos to backs of "O" and "E" panels. Open hinged "L" and "V" panels; adhere photos inside. ■

SOURCES: Papers from Bazzill and K&Company; stickers from K&Company; hinges and wire clips from Making Memories; heart brads from Provo Craft.

Love is at Your Door

DESIGN BY LINDA BEESON

Remind your sweetheart that you're thinking of him on Valentine's Day (and all throughout the year) with a special welcome greeting. A variety of lettering styles add to the unique design.

MATERIALS
Wooden door hanger
Printed paper: "Romance novel," complementary tan/brown
Black card stock
Plain white paper *or* card stock
3¾ x 4-inch fleur-de-lis foam stamp
Script background stamp
Black ink pad
Black solvent ink pad
Craft paints: mustard, cream
Crackle medium
Rub-on transfers: alphabet, "now and forever"
½-inch flat button
Silk flower
Mini key charms
Mini Scrabble tiles to spell "ALWAYS"
Epoxy alphabet tiles to spell "KISS"
Ribbons
Black-and-white check bias binding
2⅞ x 5-inch primitive heart template (optional)
Paintbrushes
Paper glue
Adhesive foam tape
Craft cement

Paint door hanger mustard; brush with one coat crackle medium. Let dry. Paint all surfaces cream; cracks will appear.

Using mustard paint as ink, stamp fleur-de-lis off right edge of door hanger. Using black solvent ink pad, stamp script background on door hanger, overlapping fleur-de-lis. Transfer "now and forever" onto painted, stamped surface.

Glue romance novel printed paper to black card stock; using heart template, cut heart from paper/card-stock layers. Rub edges over black ink pad.

Transfer letters for "LOVE" onto tan/brown paper; trim rectangles around letters and adhere to heart using paper glue. Transfer letters for "YOU" to heart below "LOVE."

Fold ribbon in a loop; adhere at bottom of heart using craft cement. Top with silk flower and button. Adhere heart to bottom of door hanger using adhesive foam tape.

Tie ribbons and bias binding through opening in door hanger; tie key charms onto bottom ribbon.

Adhere mini Scrabble tiles to spell "ALWAYS" up bottom right edge of door hanger using craft adhesive; adhere epoxy tiles to spell "KISS" in upper right corner. ■

SOURCES: Printed paper from Two Busy Moms/Deluxe Designs; fleur-de-lis stamp, paint and crackle medium from Plaid; solvent ink pad from Tsukineko; background stamp from Art Impressions; rub-on transfers from Creative Imaginations and Labelmaker; bias binding from Wrights.

St. Patrick's Treat Set

DESIGN BY LINDA BEESON

Spread Irish cheer with this quick and easy treat set filled to the top with your favorite St. Patrick's Day goodies!

TREAT BOX

Project note: Adhere pieces using a glue stick or paper glue unless instructed otherwise.

Carefully take favor box apart; lay flat. Trace around box onto back of striped paper; cut out. Adhere paper to favor box; reassemble box.

Rub 2-inch shamrock transfer onto white card stock; rub ⅜-inch shamrock transfer over larger one. Cut out, leaving narrow border. Adhere shape onto dark green card stock; cut out, leaving narrow border.

Use computer to generate, or hand-print, "think green!" on white card stock to fit within 13/16-inch square; cut out. Adhere to dark green card stock; cut out, leaving narrow border. Adhere square to shamrock. Adhere shamrock to box using adhesive foam tape.

Fill small plastic bag with candies. Tie bag shut with ribbon, catching balloons in the bow. Place bag of candies in box. ∎

SOURCES: Paper from My Mind's Eye; rub-on transfers from Royal & Langnickel.

TREAT BAG

Cut 5¾ x 5¼-inch piece dark green card stock; fold in half to form 5¾ x 2⅝-inch tag. Position tag with fold at top. Cut 5½ x 2⅜-inch rectangle from printed paper; center and adhere to tag.

Use computer to generate, or hand-print, "Happy St. Patrick's Day" in green ink on white card stock to fit within 4⅜ x 1⅛-inch rectangle; cut out. Adhere to dark green card stock; cut out, leaving narrow border. Center and adhere printed rectangle to tag. Apply shamrock stickers to tag.

Fill plastic bag with candies. Slide tag over top of bag; secure with two staples near bottom edge. ∎

SOURCES: Printed paper from KI Memories; stickers from Mrs. Grossman's.

MATERIALS

3 x 4⅝ x 2¼-inch favor box
Green striped paper
Card stock: dark green, white
Shamrock rub-on transfers: 2-inch, ⅜-inch
⅝-inch-wide green polka-dot ribbon
Small plastic bag
Green balloons
Green candies
Craft knife
Glue stick *or* paper glue
Double-sided adhesive foam tape
Computer (optional)
Computer font (optional)

MATERIALS

Printed paper
Card stock: dark green, white
Shamrock stickers
Small plastic self-sealing bag
Green candies
Stapler
Glue stick *or* paper glue
Computer (optional)
Computer font (optional)

Wearing of the Green

DESIGN BY SUSAN STRINGFELLOW

An old Irish tune inspired the design of this altered CD. The acrylic shamrocks add a bit of whimsy!

Project Note: Adhere pieces using craft cement, unless instructed otherwise.

Sand CD so that paint and glue will adhere. Paint CD cream; when dry, stamp across top using decorative rubber stamp and olive chalk ink.

Lay CD on wrong side of printed paper. Trace around CD and cut paper to cover all but top inch of the CD; adhere paper to CD. Adhere a torn 2½-inch square of embossed paper over lower left quadrant; trim edges even. Rub CD, including embossed paper, over light brown ink pad.

Wrap wire around CD about 1 inch from top; secure ends on back using adhesive tape. Thread green glass beads onto another 5-inch piece of wire; twist beaded wire onto first piece, coiling ends around a nail or large needle.

MATERIALS
Blank or recycled CD
Vintage St. Patrick's Day printed paper
Green embossed paper
Beige card stock
Decorative rubber stamp
Lowercase alphabet stamps
Ink pads: black, light brown
Olive green chalk ink pad
Cream craft paint
Cork letters
3 green acrylic shamrocks
Green glass beads
⅝-inch oval buckle
Bronze craft wire
Ribbons: ⅜-inch-wide green check, ⅛-inch-wide light green
Adhesive-backed magnet strips
Fine-grit sandpaper
Paintbrush
Nail *or* large needle
⅛-inch circle punch
Craft cement
Adhesive tape

Cut six or more 3-inch pieces of wire; use three to wire acrylic shamrocks to first wire, coiling ends around nail or large needle; adhere shamrocks to CD. Coil remaining wires around first wire. Knot green and green check ribbons onto shamrock stems and first wire.

Thread green check ribbon through oval buckle; adhere across CD about 1½ inches from bottom; adhere ribbon ends on back. Cut a 1⅛ x ½-inch tag from beige card stock; adhere to a slightly larger tag of green embossed paper. Rub tag edges on light brown ink pad. Stamp "happy" on tag using alphabet stamps and black ink pad. Punch a ⅛-inch hole in end of tag; thread 3-inch wire through hole and coil ends.

Arrange tag and cork letters to spell "st. patricks day" across bottom of CD; adhere. Lightly brush surface of letters with olive chalk ink. Adhere magnet strip to back of CD. ■

SOURCES: Printed paper from Paper Love Designs; embossed paper from Provo Craft; cork letters from LazerLetterz; decorative stamp from Stampabilities; alphabet stamps from Hero Arts; chalk ink pad from Clearsnap; buckle from Making Memories.

Magical Leprechaun Treats

DESIGN BY SUSAN STRINGFELLOW

Dress up a purchased candy dispenser with festive green paper and fibers for a quick-and-easy St. Paddy's Day treat!

Project Note: Adhere pieces using double-sided tape or paper glue unless otherwise instructed.

Adhere 1⅜ x 1-inch strip of printed paper over top of dispenser. Adhere 4½ x 1¼-inch strip of paper around top of dispenser, overlapping top strip.

Punch three ⅝-inch circles from complementary paper; adhere to front of dispenser.

Thread slider charm onto several 8-inch strands of fiber; wrap fibers around bottom edge of paper, knotting them off to one side and positioning slide charm in center. Secure fibers and charm with craft glue.

Stamp "magical leprechaun treats" onto printed paper using alphabet stamps. Stamp dragonfly in center of lower paper circle on dispenser. ■

SOURCES: Printed papers from KI Memories; alphabet stamps from Hero Arts; slider charm from Pure Allure Inc.

MATERIALS

Lime green breath mints in plastic dispenser box
Printed papers
Alphabet rubber stamps
Small dragonfly rubber stamp
Black pigment ink pad
Silver slider charm with green "jewel"
Decorative fibers
5/8-inch circle punch
Double-sided tape *or* paper glue
Craft glue

Irish Paper Quilt

DESIGN BY MARY AYRES

Pay tribute to your family heritage this St. Patrick's Day with a fun paper wall hanging. Machine stitching adds to the quilted look!

MATERIALS

8½ x 11-inch card stock:
  2 textured light green,
  2 solid light green, bright green, dark green, white, metallic gold
Green mulberry paper
5 x 7-inch photo
Green ink pad
Metallic gold craft paint
4 gold photo corners
2 (³/₁₆-inch) gold eyelets and eyelet-setting tool
11 gold mini brads
6 assorted gold buttons
9½-inch (¼-inch-diameter) wooden dowel
10 inches ½-inch-wide bright green ribbon
22 inches metallic gold pearl cotton
Small sponge
Paintbrush
Shamrock paper punch
Circle punches: ¹/₁₆-inch and ³/₁₆-inch
Sewing machine and gold metallic thread
Permanent adhesive
Computer with photo printer and scanner (optional)
Computer fonts (optional)

Adhere sheets of textured green card stock to each other in a double layer. Using sewing machine threaded with gold thread, straight-stitch around card stock ⅛ inch from edge.

Print photo on solid light green card stock in gray scale. **Option:** *Have photo reproduced at a photography studio.* Trim photo to 4¾ x 6¼ inches; using a dry sponge, rub edges with green ink. Cut metallic gold card stock 5¼ x 6¾ inches; center and adhere photo to card stock. Adhere photo panel to quilt ⅞ inch from left edge and 1⅛ inches from top and bottom.

Use computer to generate, or hand-print, "kiss me" and "i'm irish" on white card stock to fit within rectangles 1 inch tall; use a different font for each letter. Cut out rectangles leaving ⅞ inch at each end. Adhere rectangles to green mulberry paper; tear around edges. Measure rectangles; for each, cut a rectangle from dark green card stock ⅝ inch wider and taller. Center and adhere mulberry rectangles to dark green card stock. Adhere panels to top and bottom of quilt, positioning "kiss me" at top toward left and "i'm irish" at bottom toward right.

Use computer to generate, or hand-print, "Happy St. Patrick's Day" on bright green card stock to fit within 7¾ x 1¼-inch rectangle. Cut out; using a dry sponge, rub edges with green ink. Fit gold photo corners over corners; adhere to right side of quilt.

Punch 11 shamrocks from bright green card stock. Adhere shamrock to each end of white rectangle; scatter remaining shamrocks across bottom of photo. Punch a ¹/₁₆-inch hole in the center of each shamrock; fit mini brads through holes.

Adhere buttons in a cluster in bottom right corner of photo.

HANGER

Paint dowel gold; set aside to dry.

Punch a ³/₁₆-inch hole in each top corner of quilt; set eyelets in holes. Cut ribbon in half. Thread one piece through one eyelet from front to back; form into hanging loop. Adhere ribbon ends to back of quilt. Repeat on other side of quilt. Thread dowel through ribbon loops; adhere loops to dowel.

Knot ends of gold pearl cotton together; fray ends to form tassel; trim. Loop pearl cotton over ends of dowel, positioning tassel at center top of hanging cord. ∎

SOURCES: Shamrock punch from EK Success; Fabri-Tac permanent adhesive from Beacon.

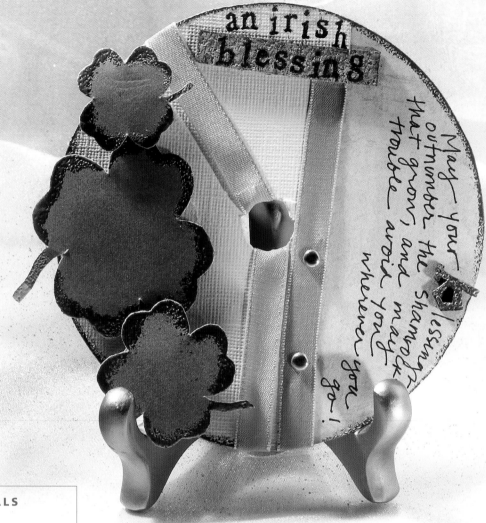

MATERIALS
Blank CD
Printed paper *or* card stock:
   pale green, textured white
Green card stock
Alphabet rubber stamps
Black solvent ink pad
Embossing ink
Gold embossing powder
Cork accents: 2 x $^3/_8$-inch
   strip, $^7/_8$-inch "b"
2 gold mini brads
Adhesive-backed magnet
   strip
Fine-tip black permanent
   marker
Green ribbon
Fine-grit sandpaper
Embossing heat tool
Craft knife
Glue stick
Craft glue
Transparent tape
Adhesive foam squares

An Irish Blessing

DESIGN BY SAHILY BEADE

An altered CD with an Irish blessing and a few shamrocks attached for good luck make a fun holiday gift!

   Sand CD so that glue will adhere. Trace around CD onto white textured paper; cut out and adhere to cover left two-thirds of CD using glue stick. Cover remainder of CD with pale green paper. Using craft knife, trim out hole in center.
   Cut green ribbon to fit across CD. Attach mini brads to one piece. Adhere ribbons, securing ends on back with tape.

Using patterns provided, cut shamrocks from green card stock. Rub edges with embossing ink; sprinkle with gold embossing powder and emboss. Mount shamrocks on left side of CD on stacks of adhesive foam squares, varying the number of squares in each stack so that shamrocks sit at different heights.

Using black ink pad and alphabet rubber stamps, stamp "blessing" on cork strip and "an irish" along top edge of CD. Adhere "blessing" strip below "an irish" using craft glue.

Ink surface of cork "b" with embossing ink; sprinkle with gold embossing powder and emboss. Using fine-tip black marker, write the following verse down right side of CD, leaving room to adhere the cork "b" for the "b" in "blessings":

May your blessings outnumber the shamrocks that grow, and may trouble avoid you wherever you go!

Adhere cork "b" using craft glue. Adhere magnet strip to back of CD. ∎

SOURCES: Printed papers from Sweetwater and Creative Imaginations; rubber stamps from Duncan; solvent ink from Tsukineko Inc.; cork accents from LazerLetterz.

PATTERNS ON PAGE 161

Gilded Shamrocks

DESIGN BY SANDY ROLLINGER

These lightweight clay pins will make stunning fashion accessories this St. Patrick's Day!

For each pin, dust candy mold with cornstarch using soft, round brush; remove excess. Press a ball of paper-based clay into mold; pop out shamrock. Let dry overnight.

Paint shamrock green. When dry, apply clear embossing ink to shamrock using craft brush; sprinkle with gold or silver embossing powder and emboss.

Wrap wire around shamrock and curl ends as desired using round-nose pliers. Secure wire as needed using craft cement. Snap shank off button; adhere button in center of shamrock, over wires, using craft cement. Adhere pin back on back of shamrock. ∎

SOURCES: Clay from Creative Paperclay Co.; Glass, Metal & More craft cement from Beacon.

MATERIALS
White air-dry paper-based clay
Emerald green pearlescent paint
Clear embossing ink
Embossing powder: gold, silver
24-gauge wire: gold, silver (optional)
Gold and silver Celtic-style shank buttons
1½-inch shamrock candy molds
1-inch pin backs
Cornstarch
Embossing heat tool
Soft round craft brush
Paintbrush
Craft brush
Round-nose pliers
Craft cement

Easter Take-Out

DESIGNS BY MARY AYRES

Charming little baskets filled with Easter treats will delight tiny tots. An easy-to-follow pattern makes creating these a snap!

Project Notes: Half of pattern is presented. Flip pattern along dotted line to draw other half. Do not fold watercolor paper along dotted line.

While card stock may be substituted for the watercolor paper, the baskets will not be as sturdy.

Adhere pieces using permanent adhesive unless instructed otherwise.

DUCK BASKET

Using pattern provided, cut basket from watercolor paper, using decorative-edge scissors to cut top edge. Score basket along dashed lines. Fold in sides and tabs.

Punch ⅛-inch hole in center of each side, near edge. Set eyelets in holes. Using dry sponge, rub scalloped edges with purple ink.

Cut 1⅞ x 2⅞-inch rectangle from lavender card stock. Using dry sponge, rub edges with purple ink.

Print duck image from CD-ROM onto photo paper. **Option:** *Use Easter stickers or images from magazines or greeting cards.* Cut out; adhere to center of lavender rectangle.

Working on one side at a time, dab jewel glue along edges of lavender rectangle and decorative edges of basket using dry sponge. Quickly sprinkle with ultrafine glitter; tap off excess.

Adhere lavender rectangle to green card stock. Using decorative-edge scissors, trim edges. Glue panel to front of basket. Punch ¹⁄₁₆-inch holes in corners of lavender rectangle. Set brads in holes.

Assemble basket, adhering side tabs to basket front and back.

Thread ends of one piece of wire through eyelets in sides of basket; twist 1 inch at each end to hold wire in place. Shape wire into handle.

For tag on handle, use computer to generate, or hand-print, Easter message onto green card stock. Cut rectangle around words, leaving space on left end for eyelet. Using dry sponge, rub edges with purple ink.

Using dry sponge, dab jewel glue along edges of tag. Quickly sprinkle with ultrafine glitter; tap off excess.

Punch a ⅛-inch hole in left end of tag. Set eyelet in hole. Thread lavender ribbon through eyelet; tie to handle in a bow. Adhere other end of tag to handle as shown.

BUNNY BASKET

Follow instructions for Duck Basket, substituting blue ink for purple; blue card stock for lavender; bunny image for duck; and blue ribbon for lavender. ■

SOURCES: Easter images CD-ROM from The Vintage Workshop; Gem-Tac jewel glue and Fabri-Tac permanent adhesive from Beacon.

PATTERNS ON PAGE 163

MATERIALS
Both Baskets

140-lb cold-press watercolor paper *or* white card stock, at least 11 inches square (see Project Notes)

Card stock: pastel lavender, green, blue

Photo paper

Vintage Easter images on CD-ROM (optional)

Ink pads: purple and blue

Iridescent ultrafine glitter

4 (⅛-inch) silver eyelets *and* eyelet-setting tool

8 silver mini brads

2 (11-inch) pieces 20-gauge tinned copper wire

¼-inch-wide gingham-check ribbon: ⅜ yard each lavender *and* blue

Decorative-edge scissors

Circle punches: ⅛-inch, ¹⁄₁₆-inch

Small sponge

Jewel glue

Permanent adhesive

Computer (optional)

Computer font (optional)

MATERIALS
Large basket
Printed *and* solid-color
   papers
Stickers
Markers
Watercolors
Florist foam
Real *or* imitation grass
Wooden skewers
Die-cutting machine with
   bird, bunny, egg, daisy,
   tulip and oval dies
Adhesive cartridge and
   applicator system

Easter Basket Centerpiece

DESIGN BY JENNIFER NARDONE, COURTESY OF ELLISON

Brightly colored die-cut bunnies, chicks and eggs planted in a basket of grass make an ideal focal point for your Easter buffet.

Line bottom of basket with florist foam. Place real or imitation grass over foam to fill basket.

Using die-cutting machine and dies, cut Easter shapes in matching pairs from printed and solid-color papers. Embellish shapes as desired, decorating ovals to look like Easter eggs.

Sandwich skewer between each pair of matching die-cuts; adhere using adhesive cartridge. Arrange die cuts in basket.

Cut narrow strips from assorted papers; coil tightly around pencil. Arrange paper coils around edge of basket. ■

SOURCES: Papers from Canson and Making Memories; additional papers and die-cutting machine and dies from Ellison/Sizzix; adhesive cartridge and applicator system from Xyron.

Mosaic Cross

DESIGN BY MARY AYRES

A ready-made embossed cross becomes a beautiful work of art with textured paper tiles and glaze.

Lightly sand cross; paint all surfaces lilac. Brush pearlescent purple paint on embossed detail; using dampened paper towel, quickly wipe off excess, leaving color in crevices.

Mix equal parts lilac paint and texturizing medium. Using sponge, dab mixture onto front and sides of frame, avoiding embossed detail, to give cross a textured appearance.

Cut tiles in random shapes from printed papers. Beginning at ends and working toward center, position tiles on cross, leaving space between them. Using paper glue, adhere tiles to cross. Paint a single heavy coat of paper glaze over each tile. Let dry overnight.

Dry-brush embossed detail and edges of cross with metallic silver paint. Attach hanger to back of cross. ∎

SOURCES: Texturizing medium and acrylic paint from DecoArt; Aleene's Paper Glaze from Duncan.

MATERIALS

7 x 11-inch flat wooden cross
    with embossed detail
Printed papers with
    "texture" patterns:
    light blue, bright blue,
    lavender, green
Acrylic paints: lilac,
    pearlescent purple
Metallic silver paint
Texturizing medium
Fine-grit sandpaper
Bristle paintbrushes
Small sponge
Paper towels
Hanger with mounting
    hardware
Paper glue
Paper glaze

Striped Bunny Box

DESIGN BY CRAFT MARKETING CONNECTIONS INC.

Painted wooden pieces combine to make cute bunnies and eggs on this Easter treat box. Fibers and eyelets add a fun embellishment.

MATERIALS

Printed papers: multicolored stripe, bright pink pin dots, light green pin dots
Wooden cutout shapes: 8 ($^3/_8$ x $^7/_8$-inch) teardrops, 4 ($^7/_8$ x 2-inch) teardrops, 20 ($^3/_8$-inch) circles, 8 ($^3/_4$-inch) circles
Crinkled purple paper shreds
Acrylic paints: white, blue, orange, lavender, bright pink
18 ($^1/_8$-inch) light green eyelets and eyelet-setting tool
Fibers: 6 inches each lavender, green, orange, pink; 32 inches multicolor
Paintbrush
Decorative-edge scissors
$^1/_8$-inch circle punch
Fine-grit sandpaper (optional)
Embossing stylus
Ruler
Instant-dry paper glue
Hot-glue gun and glue sticks

Paint all wooden cutouts white. Then paint $^3/_8$-inch circles as follows: five blue, four orange, five lavender, and six bright pink.

If desired, use sandpaper to lightly sand edges of white cutouts for a distressed look.

BOX

Lay 12-inch square of striped paper facedown; mark paper into nine equal squares as indicated on diagram. Using ruler and embossing stylus, score along drawn lines. Fold right third of paper toward center along scored line; unfold. In same manner, fold left third, bottom third and top third toward center, unfolding each time.

Referring to diagram, cut along dashed lines. Center square will be bottom of box. Fold up square 1 to form right side of box; fold in square 2 to form second side. Repeat with squares 3 and 4, 5 and 6, and 7 and 8. Using instant-dry glue, adhere overlapping sides.

Cut four 4-inch squares of light green pin-dot paper. Using instant-dry glue, adhere inside box along sides and bottom.

Cut 1½ x 12-inch and 1½ x 4-inch strips from bright pink pin-dot paper. Using decorative-edge scissors, trim strips along 4-inch and 12-inch sides. Using instant-dry glue, adhere strips around top edge of box.

Punch four ⅛-inch circles in each side of box ½ inch from top edge: ½ inch, 1½ and 2 inches from left edge, and ½ inch from right edge. Set eyelets in holes. Thread multicolored fiber through eyelets around box; tie ends in a bow at one eyelet on left edge of one side.

BUNNIES

Hot-glue ¾-inch white wooden circle to point of 2-inch teardrop for bunny head and body. Hot-glue points of two ⅞-inch teardrops behind head for ears. Hot-glue ¾-inch white circle to back of body at bottom right edge for tail. Wrap 6-inch fiber around bunny's neck; knot. Repeat to make three more bunnies.

ASSEMBLY

Hot-glue a bunny and five ⅜-inch circles to each side of box. Fill box with paper shreds. ■

SOURCES: Printed papers from Provo Craft and Making Memories; Woodsies wooden cutouts from Forster; Zip Dry instant-dry paper glue from Beacon.

DIAGRAM ON PAGE 160

Easter Treat Basket

DESIGN BY KATHLEEN PANEITZ

MATERIALS
- 5 x 4 x 3⅛-inch wooden crate basket
- Printed paper
- Paper Easter bunny
- Easter license plate
- 2 pink mini brads
- Purple wire
- Pink beads
- Acrylic paints: white, light green
- Purple crinkled paper shreds
- Fine-grit sandpaper
- Foam paintbrush
- Pencil with new eraser
- Decorative-edge scissors
- Wire cutters
- Matte decoupage medium
- Glue lines

A cheerful little bunny is dropping by with a basket of treats to wish you a Happy Easter!

Sand basket; paint light green. When dry, use pencil eraser to stamp basket with dots of white paint. Brush painted basket with decoupage medium.

Cut pieces of printed paper to line sides of basket and protrude ½ inch above rim. Trim top edge of each piece with decorative-edge scissors. Adhere glue lines inside basket at top and bottom; press paper pieces against glue lines to adhere.

Insert pink mini brads through holes in license plate. Adhere license plate and bunny to front of basket using glue lines.

Wrap end of purple wire around base of handle. Thread beads onto wire and spiral wire around handle, spacing beads. Wrap wire around base of handle at other end; trim excess. Fill basket with paper shreds. ■

SOURCES: Paper from Creative Imaginations; Easter bunny from Westrim Crafts; license plate from Junkitz; decoupage medium from Plaid; glue lines from Glue Dots International.

Pastel Egg Ornaments

DESIGNS BY LORINE MASON

Create eye-catching Easter ornaments with coordinating papers and a simple paper-folding technique.

MATERIALS
2⁷/₁₆-inch x 1¹³/₁₆-inch plastic foam eggs
Printed paper: two complementary designs/ shades of one color for each ornament
Silver filigree bead cap
½-inch-wide sheer ribbon in coordinating colors
Straight pins
Paper trimmer (optional)
Instant-dry paper glue

Using paper trimmer, cut papers into strips 1 inch wide x length of sheet. ***Option:*** *Use ruler and scissors.* Cut strips into 2-inch sections. Lay sections pattern side down; referring to Figs. 1–3, fold each into a triangle.

Starting at narrow end of egg, pin four triangles, alternating prints, with points meeting on narrow end of egg. Insert pin at each point and each end of each triangle. Paper should conceal plastic foam.

Beginning ¼ inch above point of first triangle, pin a second row of triangles around egg, pinning the first triangle in the second row between the points of two triangles in the first row. Conceal pins in first row under triangles in second row.

Continuing in this fashion, work up the egg, covering it in rows of paper triangles. Fold tiny pleats in ends of triangles as needed so they will lie flat.

At top (broad end) of egg, end with a row of four paper triangles with their corners folded under.

For bow, cut strips of ribbon: two 4-inch, two 3-inch, two 2½-inch, two 2-inch and one 1-inch. Overlap ends of each to form loop; push pin through center of loop, catching ends.

Push pins of 4-inch loops into top (broad end) of egg, crisscrossing loops. Add 3-inch loops, positioning them between the first two. Continue with 2½- and 2-inch loops. At very top, form loop from 1-inch piece of ribbon; push pin through overlapped ends and into top of egg.

Using instant-dry glue, adhere silver bead cap over pins at bottom (narrow end) of egg. ■

SOURCES: STYROFOAM® brand plastic foam eggs from Dow Chemical Co.; Zip Dry instant-dry paper glue from Beacon.

FIGURES ON PAGE 159

Bunny Notes

DESIGN BY BARBARA GREVE

This woven paper basket with a handmade bunny notebook makes a sweet Easter gift.

WEAVING BASKET

Cut 16–20 (12 x ½-inch-wide) strips each from solid pink and pink plaid papers, enough to cover cardboard box when woven.

Turn box upside down. Lay pink plaid strips side by side and lengthwise across box bottom so that they will extend beyond top of box when folded over short ends. Hold strips in place with straight pins; cover bottom of box completely. Weave solid pink strips through plaid strips to cover box bottom, making sure that they will extend beyond top of box when folded over long sides.

Trim five remaining pink plaid strips an inch or so longer than the long sides of the box. Weave them through the solid pink strips on one long side. Repeat on the other long side. Trim five remaining solid pink strips a little longer than short ends of the box; weave them through the pink plaid strips on ends.

Trim all sides so that edges will fit together at corners, leaving strips on long sides longer so that ends can be folded around corners and glued under shorter strips. Assemble basket, adhering strips with instant-dry glue. Trim top edge even. Slide basket off box.

STITCHING BASKET

Thread large-eye needle with pink raffia. On back top edge of basket, bring needle through first hole between woven strips, leaving ½-inch raffia tail inside basket; take needle over top edge and bring it through first hole again. Turn basket upside down. Overcast around basket over top edge, stitching through openings between strips. Adhere raffia ends inside basket with instant-dry paper glue.

Thread large-eye needle with green raffia, stitch grass along bottom of basket. Stitch through holes between strips for shorter blades; use paper piercer to make holes in strips for longer blades. Adhere raffia ends inside basket with instant-dry paper glue.

Punch a ⅛-inch hole in each end of basket, ¾ inch from top. Set yellow eyelets in holes. Twist pink and yellow wires together for handle; thread ends through eyelets and twist wire ends to secure. Trim excess. Tie yellow raffia bow around handle. Fill basket with green crinkled paper shreds.

MINI BUNNY ALBUM

For cover, cut 8 x 4-inch rectangle from white corrugated paper; fold in half, corrugated sides facing, to make 4-inch square. Using pattern provided, transfer bunny to cover, positioning tail along fold. Cut through both layers, leaving folded edge uncut.

Open cover; refold with smooth sides facing. Using pattern provided, punch three ⅛-inch holes through both layers ¼ inch from fold. Open cover; lay flat. Using paper piercer, punch holes along neck on front cover.

Using pattern provided, cut eight pages from solid white paper. Position one inside covers, aligning edge against fold; mark positions of holes with pencil. Punch ⅛-inch holes through page. Using this page as a template, punch holes in remaining pages.

Using large-eye needle and pink raffia, Backstitch collar through holes. Adhere raffia ends inside cover using instant-dry glue. Using embroidery needle and double strand of black embroidery floss, stitch French Knot through front cover for bunny's eye.

Using pattern provided, cut two cover linings, reversing one, from pink plaid paper. Adhere cover linings inside covers with permanent adhesive. Repunch holes through linings.

Stack pages inside covers. Thread large-eye needle with white raffia. Leaving a 2-inch tail, bring needle and raffia over top edge of tail and through top hole from front to back. Bring needle and raffia around edge and through center hole from front to back; repeat, stitching through bottom hole from front to back. Reverse stitching back up fold, crisscrossing stitches over fold. Knot raffia ends on back; trim. Secure knot with instant-dry glue.

Adhere pink raffia bow to bunny's collar with permanent adhesive.

EGGS

Using oval template and shape cutter, cut 1 x 1½-inch ovals from purple and white corrugated papers. Using patterns provided and paper piercer, punch holes in eggs.

Referring to photo, Backstitch designs on eggs, using pink raffia on purple egg and purple raffia on ivory egg.

CHICK

Using oval template and shape cutter, cut 1 x 1½-inch oval from yellow corrugated paper. Using patterns provided, cut two wings from solid yellow paper and beak from solid orange; trim bottom off chick following dashed line on pattern.

Adhere wings and beak to chick using instant-dry glue. Using embroidery needle and doubled strand of black embroidery floss, stitch French knots for eyes.

ASSEMBLY

Nestle bunny notebook in basket. Glue eggs and chick to basket using permanent adhesive; bend chick's wings forward. ■

SOURCES: Wire from Toner Plastics; templates and cutter from Fiskars; Zip Dry instant-dry paper glue and Fabri-Tac permanent adhesive from Beacon.

PATTERNS ON PAGE 160

MATERIALS

Small cardboard box, approximately 3 x 4 x 2½ inches

Printed papers: 12-inch sheets of pink plaid, solid pink and solid white, and scraps of solid orange and yellow

Corrugated paper: yellow, white, ivory and purple

Green crinkled paper shreds

2 (⅛-inch) yellow eyelets and eyelet-setting tool

Raffia: pink, purple, green, yellow and white

28-gauge craft wire: 23 inches each pink *and* yellow

Black embroidery floss

Straight pins

1 x 1½-inch oval template with cutter

⅛-inch punch *and* hammer

Paper piercer

Large-eye needle

Embroidery needle

Wire cutters

Pencil

Instant-dry paper glue

Permanent adhesive

Bunny Tic-Tac-Toe

DESIGN BY SANDY ROLLINGER

Have a yummy time playing a favorite childhood game when jelly beans are used as X's and O's. Winner takes all!

MATERIALS

Card stock: white, pink
White poster board
Wooden cutout shapes:
    4 (2 x $7/8$-inch) ovals,
    2 (2 x $15/16$-inch) teardrops,
    2 ($1\frac{1}{2}$ x $9/16$-inch) teardrops,
    2 ($7/8$-inch-diameter) circles,
    $7/16$-inch-diameter circle,
    2 ($1\frac{1}{8}$ x $7/8$-inch) hearts
Jelly beans for playing pieces
Acrylic paints: pink, light
    blue, white
Dimensional paints for
    paper: white, pink
2 (7mm) movable eyes
$\frac{1}{2}$-inch pink flat button
Paper crimper
Decorative-edge scissors
Paintbrushes
Instant-dry paper glue
Craft cement

Using patterns provided, cut two heads and two bodies from white card stock. Run one head and body through crimper so that "valleys" run from side to side on head and top to bottom on body.

Cut one head and one body from white poster board; trim slightly smaller than card stock pieces. Adhere crimped head and body to poster board pieces using instant-dry glue.

Cut one tummy from pink card stock; trim edges using decorative-edge scissors. Adhere tummy in center of body using instant-dry glue.

Paint $7/16$-inch circle and hearts light blue; paint smaller teardrops pink; paint remaining cutouts white.

Using craft cement throughout, adhere two ovals at bottom of body for hind feet; adhere remaining ovals partially behind body near top for front paws. Adhere hearts at chin, points touching, for bow tie; adhere $7/16$-inch circle over points. Adhere $7/8$-inch circles to face, edges touching, for cheeks; adhere pink button over circles. Adhere movable eyes to face, touching cheeks. Adhere pink teardrops to white teardrops; adhere teardrops behind head for ears.

Glue remaining card stock head and body to back of bunny using instant-dry glue. Outline feet, paws, cheeks and white ears with squiggly lines of pink dimensional paint; add dots to feet, paws and cheeks.

Draw squiggly lines of white dimensional paint on tummy for playing board; add squiggly outline around center and loops of bow tie.

Play tic-tac-toe on bunny's tummy using jelly beans for playing pieces. The winner gets to eat all the jelly beans! ■

SOURCES: Woodsies wooden shapes from Forster; dimensional paints from Plaid; Zip Dry instant-dry paper glue and Glass, Metal & More craft cement from Beacon.

PATTERNS ON PAGE 161

Happy Mother's Day

Mom, Thank you for being a wonderful mother. Without you having been such a caring and loving mom to me, I wouldn't be able to pass that on to your beautiful, su... love will shine through... with her favorite d...

A Mother is Love

A Mother Is Love

DESIGN BY MELISSA SMITH

Create a lovely scrapbook page to display standing on an easel or hanging on the wall. A lovely card announces this gift in coordinating style.

MATERIALS
Printed papers: brown floral, beige/green floral, pink, green
Green card stock
Green/beige wreath paper frame
Photo to fit in frame
2 paper leaf sprays
3 floral die-cut sheets
Transparency
Gold ribbon bow
Gold ribbon photo corners
Metallic rub-on finish
Double-sided tape
Computer (optional)
Computer font (optional)

FRAME LAYOUT

Project note: Adhere all pieces using double-sided tape unless instructed otherwise.

Layer brown, beige/green and pink background prints, leaving ¼-inch borders all around. Layer green printed paper on bottom one-quarter of pink background piece. Use computer to generate, or hand-print, message onto transparency; trim to fit, leaving room at top for floral die cuts. Adhere transparency to layout; adhere photo behind frame.

For "Happy Mother's Day" tag, use computer to generate, or hand-print, "Happy Mother's Day" onto transparency. Adhere 1½ x 3½-inch piece pink floral paper to green card stock; trim, leaving narrow border. Adhere transparency to top of tag at an angle, applying tape at bottom where it will be concealed by die cuts.

Arrange flower and leaf die cuts, concealing seams between background papers. Wrap one leaf spray around top of title tag; adhere. *Option: Cut apart some die cuts to permit more flexibility in arranging.*

Rub edges of papers and die cuts with metallic finish. Trim 2 inches from tails of ribbon bow; reserve for card. Adhere bow at top of frame. Adhere ribbon photo corners.

CARD

Use computer to generate, or hand-print, "A Mother Is Love" onto transparency to fit within frame. Position pink printed paper and printed transparency behind one frame; tuck in die-cut flowers; adhere.

Lay frame face up on wrong side of another sheet of pink printed paper; trace around frame and cut out; set aside. Fold 2-inch ribbon reserved from frame layout in half; sandwich ends on right edge of frame, between pink printed paper used to back card front and second pink piece cut in previous step; adhere. Write sentiment inside front cover of card.

Adhere photo behind second frame. Add "Happy Mother's Day" with computer or rub-ons, if desired.

Lay frames together; punch two holes ½ inch apart and ½ inch from left edge. Thread tails of bow through holes; knot on back so card will open and close. ∎

SOURCE: Printed paper, frames, leaf sprays, die-cut sheets, ribbon bows and photo corners from Anna Griffin Inc.

MATERIALS
Pink printed paper
2 green/beige wreath paper frames
Photo to fit in frame
Floral die-cut sheet
Transparency
Gold ribbon bow
Reserved ribbon from bow for frame layout
Alphabet rub-on transfers (optional)
Fine-tip marker or pen
Circle punch
Double-sided tape
Computer (optional)
Computer font (optional)

Spring Renewal

DESIGN BY EILEEN HULL

MATERIALS
Small candle in clear glass votive holder
Blue floral printed paper
White vellum
Transparency
Ultrafine glitter
½ x ¼-inch clear acrylic tile
Light green eyelet and eyelet-setting tool
Silver craft wire
⅛-inch circle punch
1¾-inch tag punch
1¾-inch square punch
Sandpaper
Glue pen
Double-sided tape
Instant decoupage glue
Computer (optional)
Computer font (optional)

The softly flickering light of a tea-light candle shines through the vellum inserts of a very feminine candle screen.

Project note: *Do not place candle inside screen without a glass candle cup.*

Cut 9½ x 2¼-inch strip printed paper; score every 2¼ inches. Fold strip into box shape, leaving tab for adhering later. Punch 1¾-inch square in center of each panel. Adhere a 2-inch square of vellum behind each "window" using double-sided tape.

Outline flowers on paper using glue pen; sprinkle with glitter. Assemble candle screen, adhering tab using double-sided tape. Punch ⅛-inch hole for attaching tag in upper left corner of one panel.

Punch tag from printed paper, using reverse side of paper for right side of tag. Sand edges. Use computer to generate, or hand-print, message on transparency to fit within ¹⁵⁄₁₆ x 1³⁄₁₆-inch rectangle; cut out and adhere to tag using instant decoupage glue. Cover one word in message with acrylic tile; adhere using instant decoupage glue.

Punch ⅛-inch hole in top of tag; mount eyelet in hole. Attach tag to screen, threading small coil of wire through holes. Set small votive candle in clear glass cup inside screen. ■

SOURCES: Printed paper from Making Memories; acrylic tile from Heidi Grace Designs; punches from EK Success; decoupage glue from Duncan.

Butterflies & Beads Votive

DESIGN BY SANDY ROLLINGER

A simple strip of crimped vellum becomes an eye-catching accent when embellished with beads and a butterfly.

Clean votive with glass cleaner and soft cloth. Spray with three coats frosting finish, letting finish dry between coats.

Cut 1½-inch-wide strip of vellum long enough to go around votive and overlap. Trim long edges with decorative-edge scissors. Run vellum through crimper; test fit and trim overlap to ½ inch. Adhere vellum around votive, applying dots of craft cement to votive and to overlap using a toothpick.

Roll paper-based clay flat on parchment paper using rolling pin. Dip butterfly cookie cutter in cornstarch, then cut butterfly from clay. Let butterfly dry for a few hours; paint butterfly lilac.

Curl one end of 8-inch piece of wire using round-nose pliers. String pearls and glass beads onto wire, alternating three pearls and glass bead. Curl other end of wire. Wrap wire around votive over parchment strip; twist ends together in a decorative "S" shape. Apply dots of cement to backs of some glass beads to hold wire in place.

Fold a 3-inch piece of wire in half; curl ends for antennae. Thread three glass beads onto wire for butterfly body. Apply cement to hold beads in place. Let dry for 5 minutes, then adhere butterfly to votive to the right of twisted wire ends. ∎

SOURCES: Clay from Creative Paperclay Co.; frosted glass finish from Krylon; craft cement from Beacon.

MATERIALS

White paper-based
  air-dry clay
White vellum
3- to 4-inch candle jar
  or glass votive with
  straight sides
Frosting finish for glass
Lilac craft paint
Glass tube beads: green,
  blue, turquoise
3.5mm white pearl beads
24-gauge silver wire
Glass cleaner
Soft cloth
Parchment paper
1¼-inch butterfly
  cookie cutter
Cornstarch
Decorative-edge scissors
Paper crimper
Rolling pin or brayer
Toothpick
Paintbrush
Round-nose pliers
Wire cutters
Craft cement

Tea-Time Desk Set

DESIGNS BY LISA ROJAS

This lovely coordinating set includes a stationery box (complete with handmade cards), an address book, a birdhouse note clip, a pen cup and even matching pens. What a great gift for Mom!

STATIONERY BOX

Cover cigar box and lid, including edges, with dark green mulberry paper, adhering with gel tacky glue applied with foam brush. Line interior of box with light green mulberry paper.

Using a craft knife, cut foam-core board ¼ inch smaller than box lid; cut 4-inch-square window in upper left corner of foam-core board. Cover foam-core board, including outer edges, with light green mulberry paper.

Cut two 4¼-inch squares acetate; adhere one over window on back of foam-core board. Punch five teapots from pink handmade paper; place in window with dried potpourri. Adhere remaining acetate square over front of window.

Cut tan card stock slightly smaller than foam-core board; stamp sprig randomly over card stock using olive green ink pad. Cut window in upper left corner slightly smaller than window in foam-core board. Run card stock through adhesive applicator; adhere on top of foam-core board. Hot-glue foam-core board to box lid.

Using hot-glue gun, adhere jacquard ribbon around edges of window, edges of foam-core panel, top edge of box, and inside box over edge of light green lining; adhere twisted cord around top of lid, beginning and ending at center front; adhere frog closure to lid and box; adhere ribbon roses to window corners and frog closure.

NOTE CARDS

Form note cards from cream card stock to fit in envelopes; trim edges with decorative-edge scissors, if desired.

Stamp background image onto white card stock using olive

or dark green ink pad; color with watercolor pencils. Spray stamped image with sealer. Run stamped image through adhesive applicator; adhere to dark or light green mulberry paper; tear around edges. Adhere mulberry paper to front of

MATERIALS

Textured card stock:
   white, cream
Mulberry paper: dark green,
   light green
6½ x 4¾-inch cream
   envelopes
Rubber stamps: floral
   background, floral sprig
Chalk ink pads: olive green,
   dark green
Watercolor pencils
³/₈-inch-wide ribbon:
   cream, green
1¼-inch-wide green ribbon
Decorative-edge scissors
   (optional)
Adhesive applicator with
   adhesive cartridge
Spray sealer

MATERIALS

Cigar box
Foam-core board
Mulberry paper: dark green,
   light green
Pink handmade paper
Tan card stock
Clear acetate
Floral sprig rubber stamp
Chalk ink pads: olive green,
   dark green
5 ribbon roses
Cream twisted cord
³/₈-inch-wide cream
   jacquard ribbon
Satin cord "frog" closure
Dried potpourri
Foam brush
Teapot punch
Craft knife
Gel tacky glue
Adhesive applicator with
   adhesive cartridge
Hot-glue gun and glue sticks

MATERIALS

Ring binder address book
Green mulberry paper
Pink handmade paper
White card stock
5 lace medallions
Rubber stamps: floral
    background, floral sprig
Chalk ink pads: olive green,
    dark green
Watercolor pencils
1½-inch-wide green
    sheer ribbon
Foam brush
Gel tacky glue
Adhesive applicator with
    adhesive cartridge
Hot-glue gun and glue sticks
Spray sealer

MATERIALS

Small straight-sided plastic
    container, like 2-inch
    pill bottle
Gel pens
White cardboard
Pink handmade paper
Photo to fit frame
Rubber stamps: teapot
    frame, floral sprig
Dark green chalk ink pad
Black pigment ink pad
Clear embossing powder
Watercolor pencils
³/₈-inch-wide sheer
    green ribbon
Pearl bead trim
Glitter
Spray sealer
Paper glaze
Paintbrush
Embossing heat tool
Teapot punch
Craft knife
Double-sided tape
Adhesive applicator with
    adhesive cartridge
Adhesive dots
Hot-glue gun and glue sticks

note card. Tie ⅜-inch ribbon in a bow; adhere near top of stamped design. Repeat to make desired number of note cards.

Stamp envelopes using sprig rubber stamp and olive green ink pad. Tie note cards and envelopes in a bundle with 1¼-inch green ribbon.

ADDRESS BOOK

Cover address book, inside and out, using pink handmade paper. Stamp sprig randomly over book using olive green ink pad.

Stamp background image onto white card stock using dark green ink pad; color with watercolor pencils. Spray stamped image with sealer. Cut out stamped image; run through adhesive applicator; adhere to green mulberry paper; tear around edges. Adhere mulberry paper to front of address book.

Run lace medallions through adhesive applicator; adhere to address book. Tie ribbon in bow around spine of address book.

NOTE HOLDER

Paint dowel, clothespin, spool and roof of birdhouse green; paint birdhouse pink. Cut pink handmade paper to fit around spool; stamp sprig in center using dark green ink pad. Run stamped paper through adhesive applicator; adhere around spool.

Stamp birdhouse with sprig. Spray birdhouse, dowel and clothespin with sealer. Drill shallow ¼-inch hole in bottom of birdhouse; hot-glue one end of dowel in hole; hot-glue other end in spool.

Punch one teapot from pink handmade paper; hot-glue to bottom half of clothespin, taking care not to glue clothespin closed. Hot-glue clothespin on top of spool. Hot-glue dried flowers to dowel; tie green ribbon in a bow around dowel.

PEN HOLDER & PENS

Stamp teapot frame twice onto white cardboard using black ink pad. Sprinkle with clear embossing powder; emboss. Color images with watercolor pencils; spray with sealer. Cut out teapots using a craft knife. Cut out frame openings and opening in handle from one image only.

Hot-glue pearl trim around edges of front image (the one with cutout openings). Adhere photo behind frame using double-sided tape. Adhere front teapot to back teapot using adhesive dots. Brush a thin layer of paper glaze on front teapot, avoiding photo.

Cut pink handmade paper to fit around plastic container; stamp paper with floral sprig using dark green ink pad. Run stamped paper through adhesive applicator and adhere to plastic container. Hot-glue ribbon around container's top and bottom edges; hot-glue container to back of frame so that frame will stand.

For pens, punch a pink teapot from pink handmade paper for each pen; adhere at top of pen using adhesive dots. Wrap double-sided tape around pen in a spiral; sprinkle with glitter. ■

MATERIALS

Small wooden birdhouse
4½-inch (¼-inch-diameter)
    wooden dowel
1⅝-inch x 1½-inch-diameter
    wooden spool
2¾-inch spring clothespin
Pink handmade paper
Floral sprig rubber stamp
Dark green chalk ink pad
Craft paints: pink, green
³/₈-inch-wide green sheer
    ribbon
Dried flowers
Teapot punch
Paintbrush
Adhesive applicator with
    adhesive cartridge
Hot-glue gun and glue sticks
Spray sealer
Drill with ¼-inch bit

SOURCES: Rubber stamps from Delta/Rubber Stampede and Embossing Arts; chalk ink pads from Stampa Rosa; gel tacky glue and paper glaze from Duncan; permanent adhesive cartridges and applicator from Xyron.

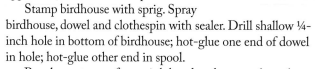

A mother holds a special part of all that is treasured in the heart

Shadowbox Art

DESIGN BY LORINE MASON

Fill a shadowbox frame with paper cutouts that have been embellished with glitter to create an elegant gift that will be treasured by Mom.

Discard acrylic panel that comes with frame. Paint frame's inside edges with two coats light ivory; paint exterior of frame and inside back of frame with two coats light turquoise.

Thin light ivory paint with water; brush across front and outer edges of frame. Wipe off excess with a soft cloth, leaving paint in crevices.

Use computer to generate, or hand-print, "A mother holds a special part of all that is treasured in the heart" onto vellum. Cut out, centering lettering in a 4 x 3½-inch rectangle.

Adhere frame die cut in center back of frame using adhesive foam squares. Center vellum over frame; adhere using dots of paper glue in corners.

Cut between petals and leaves on flower die cuts. Curve edges of petals, leaves and butterfly wings over blade of scissors.

Adhere flower and butterfly die cuts in frame, positioning some on corners of vellum frame, and others toward front, at varying depths behind front of frame, using water-based super glue and adhesive foam squares. ■

SOURCES: Die cuts and frame from Amscan; water-based super glue from The Adhesive Products Inc.

MATERIALS
7 x 5-inch wooden
    shadowbox frame
Die cuts: flower,
    butterfly, frame
Clear vellum
Craft paints: light turquoise,
    light ivory
Soft cloth
Foam paintbrushes
Clear-drying glitter glue
Paper glue
Adhesive foam squares
Water-based super glue
Computer (optional)
Computer font (optional)

Thank You, Mom

DESIGN BY VANESSA HUDSON

Full of personal expressions of love and gratitude, this is one gift Mom will talk about for years to come.

Project notes: *Give your project a vintage look by choosing papers and card stock in "tea-dyed" hues, and by rubbing all edges and surfaces with distress ink.*

Adhere papers using paper glue or double-sided tape; use craft cement or adhesive dots for ribbons, string and charms.

Use computer to generate, or hand-print, lettering. Or, use alphabet stamps and a brown ink pad, or alphabet rub-on transfers.

ENVELOPE

Cut printed papers in pieces to cover flap side of envelope, leaving narrow borders uncovered. Using sewing machine and dark red thread 4¼ x 2⅝-inch printed paper; tear down right edges. Machine-stitch paper to card stock, leaving ½-inch margin on left edge. Print "MOM" on paper panel.

Knot ribbon around "MOM" cover. Print "Thank you" on tiny card stock tag. Punch ¹⁄₁₆-inch hole through tag; tie to ribbon with string. Adhere sticker to back of "MOM" cover. Attach cover to envelope using hinges and antique mini brads.

Print message on card stock; trim to measure 3¾ x 1¾ inches. Adhere to printed paper; trim, leaving narrow border. Adhere to envelope under "MOM" cover.

Print "to … from" information on printed paper; trim in label shape and adhere to reverse side of envelope. Embellish with stickers. Thread heart charm onto string; knot ribbon and adhere over string, at upper right corner of label.

MESSAGE STRIPS

Cut card stock strips for messages to fit in envelope. Machine-stitch printed papers over ends; add stickers and desired messages. Insert strips in envelope. ■

MATERIALS

Printed papers: 3 patterns
Pale tan card stock
4⅛ x 9⅝-inch kraft envelope
Mini tan card stock tag
Stickers
Alphabet rubber stamps
Brown ink pad
Brown distress ink
Antique heart charm
2 antique metal hinges
Antique mini brads
¾-inch-wide picot-edge
    ribbon
Fine string
¹⁄₁₆-inch circle punch
Craft knife
Sewing machine with dark
    red thread
Craft cement or adhesive dots
Paper glue or
    double-sided tape
Computer (optional)
Computer fonts (optional)

Teacups & Roses Desk Set

DESIGNS BY MARY AYRES

Handmade papers and metal corner pieces accent this attractive desk set. Add personalized stationery and packets of flavored tea for a gift Mom is sure to love.

Project note: Adhere all elements using scrapbook adhesive unless instructed otherwise.

HANDMADE PAPER

Following manufacturer's instructions, use the pour hand mold to make three sheets of paper. For each sheet, place torn pieces from a sheet of light pink card stock into a blender with ¼ teaspoon mica dust and ¼ teaspoon mica sprinkles. Iron paper dry between sheets of waxed paper. **Option:** *Substitute three sheets ready-made light pink handmade paper.*

ORGANIZER

Paint organizer white. Cut handmade paper to fit on front and back; adhere.

Fill 8½ x 11-inch sheet white card stock with images using roses border stamp and black ink pad. Color images with colored pencils. Cut pieces to fit sides of organizer; adhere. Use small dry sponge to rub edges of organizer with pink ink. Adhere small molding corners in front bottom corners of organizer.

Stamp three teacups on white cardstock using black ink pad. Color roses and leaves, and shade teacups using colored pencils. Cut out images; adhere across front of organizer using adhesive foam squares.

FRAME

Cut handmade paper to fit on front of frame; adhere. Use a small dry sponge to rub edges of frame with pink ink.

Dry-brush large page corners with white paint. Adhere corners to frame in upper left and lower right corners.

Stamp a teacup on white card stock using black ink pad. Color and shade using colored pencils. Cut out image; adhere to frame at center bottom using adhesive foam squares.

Tear a 1¼ x ½-inch strip from dark pink card stock; use small dry sponge to rub edges with pink ink. Punch ⅛-inch hole in left end; mount eyelet in hole. Adhere stickers to premade tag to spell "MOM." Thread tag and butterfly charm onto ribbon; tie around teacup handle. Trim ribbon ends. Adhere tag to frame using adhesive foam square.

BOX

Paint box white. Let dry thoroughly.

Apply vertical strips of masking tape to sides of box, side by side, until box is covered. Carefully peel off every other strip. Brush silver paint onto exposed areas. Remove remaining tape.

Cut handmade paper to fit top of lid; adhere. Use a small dry sponge to rub edges with pink ink.

Stamp one rose on white card stock using black ink pad. Color using colored pencils. Cut out image, centering it in a 2-inch square. Use a small dry sponge to rub edges with pink ink. Adhere small molding corners in corners on top of lid.

Dry-brush floral frame with white paint. Adhere rose square on back of frame. Adhere frame diagonally onto box lid. ∎

SOURCES: Papermill Pro pour hand mold, mica dust and mica sprinkles from Arnold Grummer's; organizer from Walnut Hollow; canvas frame from EK Success; metal corners from Making Memories; floral frame, charm, page corners and stickers from K&Company; rubber stamps from Plaid/All Night Media.

MATERIALS

9½ x 5⅜ x 3⅜-inch papier-mâché organizer
4-inch-square papier-mâché box with lid
5⅝ x 7¼-inch canvas picture frame
Card stock: white, dark pink
3 (8½ x 14-inch) sheets light pink card stock (optional)
Paper pour hand mold (optional)
Mica dust (optional)
Rose mica sprinkles (optional)
Rubber stamps: teacup, roses border
Ink pads: black, pink
Colored pencils
Craft paints: white, silver
Alphabet stickers
6 small metal molding corners
Floral frame
Butterfly charm
2 metal page corners
⅛-inch silver eyelet and eyelet-setting tool
Premade tag
¼-inch-wide pink checked ribbon
⅛-inch circle punch
Paintbrush
Blender (optional)
Waxed paper (optional)
Iron (optional)
Small dry sponge
¾-inch painter's masking tape
Paper glue
¼-inch adhesive foam squares

Cherished Memories

DESIGN BY LINDA BEESON

In appreciation for a lifetime of love, present your mother with a book filled with memories of happy moments.

MATERIALS
Printed paper
Card stock: white, pink textured
Small vintage photos
Assorted vintage stickers
Alphabet rubber stamps
Black ink pad
Chalk ink pads: green, pale peach
Brown distress ink
Alphabet rub-on transfers
Tiny green buttons
¾-inch safety pin
Decorative brad
Antique photo turn
Black photo corners
Mini snap
Tiny green alphabet beads
Oval "mom" page pebble
Ribbons: pink, green
Flower punches: 1-inch, ⁵⁄₈-inch
Circle punches: ¹⁄₈-inch, 1¼-inch
Decorative-edge scissors
Stapler and green staples
Paper glue
Craft cement
Computer (optional)
Computer font (optional)

Accordion-fold 12 x 4-inch strip printed paper into four sections. Rub edges with green ink chalk pad.

Panel 1: Use computer to generate, or hand-print, "thanks for the memories" on white card stock; cut into strips and rub with peach chalk ink pad. Adhere to panel using paper glue. Center tiny green buttons over three ⁵⁄₈-inch flowers punched from pink card stock; adhere over ends of card-stock strips. Staple ribbon over top left edge; use rub-on transfers and/or alphabet stamps to stamp "Mom" under strips.

Panel 2: Rub edges of photo with distress ink. Affix photo corners; adhere to panel. ***Option:*** *Cut small section from larger photo; mount on white card stock and trim edges using deckle-edge scissors to mimic the deckled edge on vintage photos.* Add stickers, rub-on transfers, and "mom" page pebble.

Panel 3: Knot ribbon onto tiny safety pin; affix to corner of photo. Punch 1-inch flower from pink card stock; set flower aside for Panel 4. Center punched negative image within punched 1½-inch circle; overlap with photo and adhere to panel. Stamp words using green chalk ink pad. Add other words and embellishments as desired.

Panel 4: Affix punched flower to panel using decorative brad. Adhere photo to panel, overlapping with antique photo turn. Stamp words using green chalk ink pad. Glue tiny alphabet beads to spell "MOM" below photo. Staple ribbon over bottom right edge of panel. ■

SOURCES: Printed paper from Autumn Leaves; rubber stamps from Hero Arts; buttons, safety pin, photo turn, mini snap and page pebble from Making Memories; stickers from Bo-Bunny Press; chalk ink pads from Clearsnap.

Mom's Button Box

DESIGN BY MARY AYRES

Create faux couture button cards to feature favorites from your mother's button box.

Remove labels from cigar box; sand. Using black ink pad, stamp button card twice onto each printed paper or card stock; cut out cards around edges. Using dry sponge, rub edges lightly with brown ink. Adhere mounting adhesive on backs of stamped cards.

Arrange cards on box lid, varying positions and colors; peel off backing sheet and adhere button cards to box lid. Using craft cement, adhere pairs of matching buttons over stamped buttons on cards.

Use computer to generate, or hand-print, "MOM'S BUTTON BOX" on yellow parchment card stock, omitting the "O's" and leaving space for ⅜-inch buttons. Cut narrow tag shape around words, leaving ⅜ inch of blank space at left end. Using sponge, rub edges with brown ink. Using sewing machine threaded with white thread, machine-stitch around tag ⅛ inch from edge.

Punch ⅛-inch hole in left end of tag; mount eyelet in hole. Using craft cement, adhere ⅜-inch buttons to tag in spaces for "O's." Thread tag and scissors charm onto string; wrap string around box several times and tie ends in a bow. ∎

SOURCES: Printed papers from Hero Arts; rubber stamp from Plaid/All Night Media.

MATERIALS
7¼ x 9¼ x 1½-inch cigar box
6 colors complementary pastel solid-look printed papers or card stock
Yellow parchment card stock
Button card rubber stamp
Ink pads: black, brown
Buttons: 3 (³/₈-inch) white shirt buttons and 12 pairs ½- to ¾-inch flat buttons
Brass scissors charm
⅛-inch antique eyelet and eyelet-setting tool
White string
Sandpaper
Small dry sponge
Sewing machine with white sewing thread
⅛-inch circle punch
Mounting adhesive sheets
Craft cement
Computer (optional)
Computer font (optional)

Climbing Flowers Plaque

DESIGN BY SANDY ROLLINGER

MATERIALS

8-inch-square tin plaque
    with handle
White handmade paper
Printed paper: blue,
    pink, yellow
Green 1/8-inch-wide paper
    quilling strips
Craft paints: white,
    light green
Dimensional paints: white,
    blue, yellow
Slotted quilling tool
1-inch flat paintbrush
Flower paper punches:
    1-inch, 2 types 5/8-inch
Alcohol
Soft cloth
Paper or foam plate
Toothpicks
Tweezers
Craft cement
Instant-dry paper glue

Embellish an antique tin plaque with handmade paper and a simple arrangement of punched paper flowers.

Clean tin plaque using alcohol and soft cloth. Paint border of plaque light green; dry-brush raised areas of tile border with white.

Cut square of white handmade paper to fit in center of plaque (approximately 5 inches). Apply water to edges using brush; gently pull away moistened paper to leave ragged edges. When dry, adhere paper square in center of plaque using craft cement.

Punch three 1-inch flowers from yellow printed paper; dot centers with blue dimensional paint. Punch three 5/8-inch flowers each from pink and blue printed papers; dots centers of pink flowers with white dimensional paint and blue flowers with yellow.

For vines, cut five 4-inch strips of green quilling paper. Curl one end of each in quilling tool.

For leaves, cut six 2-inch strips of green quilling paper. Using pattern provided, form each into a teardrop. Secure shapes using drops of instant-dry paper glue applied with a toothpick.

Referring to placement diagram, adhere vines to handmade paper square, using a toothpick to apply just enough instant-dry paper glue along one edge to adhere it. Use tweezers to position vines and hold them in place until glue sets. Adhere leaves around vines. Adhere flowers over vines and onto handmade paper. ∎

SOURCE: Instant-dry paper glue from Beacon.

PATTERN AND DIAGRAM ON PAGE 162

Golf Nostalgia

DESIGN BY LORINE MASON

Use golf balls from memorable games or favorite courses for a hole-in-one winning project.

MATERIALS
2 (5-inch-square) flat
    wooden frames
2 golf balls
2 scorecard pencils
Printed paper
Vintage golf stickers
2 (5½-inch) squares moss
    green mat board
Moss green card stock
1 yard ⅝-inch-wide warm
    brown grosgrain ribbon
Hot-glue gun and glue stick
Double-sided adhesive sheet
Adhesive foam squares

Cover frames with printed paper, wrapping paper around edges to back and mitering corners; adhere using pieces cut from double-sided adhesive sheet. Center and hot-glue frames on mat-board squares.

Adhere stickers to card stock; cut out, leaving very narrow borders. Arrange stickers on frames; adhere, using pieces cut from double-sided adhesive sheet for some and adhesive foam squares for others.

Hot-glue golf balls in centers of frames; hot-glue pencils across upper left corners.

Fold ribbon in half. Leaving hanging loop at top, hot-glue ribbons to backs of frames, overlapping ribbon edges slightly. Trim ribbon ends at an angle. ■

SOURCE: Golf stickers from K&Company.

ALGON-KIAN G.C.
GOLF LINKS
HERNDON GOLF COURSE
THE NORMAL CHRISTIAN LIFE
WATCHMAN NEE

MATERIALS

5-inch-square, 1⅛-inch-
  deep wooden frame
Flag/patriotic printed paper
White card stock
White vellum
Vintage photo
Adhesive mesh: red, blue
Navy blue craft paint
Rub-on alphabet transfers:
  ⅛-inch, ¼-inch
Silver alphabet slide tiles to
  spell "HERO"
"USA" button nail head
4 nickel brads with loops
¼-inch-wide sheer
  red ribbon
Blue fiber
Sandpaper
Paintbrush
Paper piercer
Vellum tape
Paper glue

Hero Frame

DESIGN BY BARBARA GREVE

Salute your family's hero with a frame that highlights his life accomplishments. Dad wasn't in the service? Change the colors and embellishments to coordinate with the photo.

Sand frame; paint blue. Trace around frame onto wrong side of printed paper and card stock; cut out. Cut frame openings from both pieces. Adhere printed paper to card-stock frame.

Pierce holes for brads with loops through paper/card-stock frame below and just outside bottom corners of opening; fit brads in holes. String "HERO" slide charms on sheer red ribbon; knot ribbon ends in brad loops. Pierce frame and mount USA button nail head on right side of frame.

Use rub-on transfers to adhere "FATHER" and "Husband" on white vellum; cut strips around words. Adhere strips to top and left side of paper/card-stock frame using vellum tape. Adhere paper/card-stock frame to wooden frame using scrapbook adhesive.

Cut photo to fit in frame opening. Cut adhesive mesh: 1 x 2½ inches red, ¾ x 2½ inches red, ¾ x 3 inches blue. Cut 2¾ x 3⅛-inch strip white vellum.

Adhere photo to cardboard frame backing to fit in frame opening; adhere blue mesh down left side and red mesh across top and bottom. Adhere vellum over photo using vellum tape. Pierce two holes through all layers near left edge; fit brads in holes. Knot blue fiber between loops. Mount photo panel in frame. ■

SOURCE: Printed paper and USA button nail head from K&Company.

Best Dad

DESIGN BY EILEEN HULL

Every time your father glances in this mirror, he'll be reminded of your loving feelings for him.

Mask off mirror with scrap paper; spray mirror frame with brown paint. Stamp trees randomly over frame using brown pigment ink pad; stamp some images off edges. Ink stencil brush using brown pigment ink pad and stipple around inner and outer edges of frame, feathering paint toward middle. Spray frame with fixative.

Use computer to generate, or hand-print, "You're looking at the best dad in the world" on transparency so that it will fit around mirror opening. Add symbols, dingbats or other images as desired. Using craft knife, cut out transparency; cut opening in center for mirror. Outline transparency with gold leafing pen. Apply spray adhesive to back of transparency; adhere to frame.

Trim black mat board slightly larger than die-cut "love" stamp; mount and center stamp on mat board using adhesive foam squares. Mount mat board on rough side of sandpaper using spray adhesive; cut out leaving ⅛-inch border. Adhere stamp panel to bottom of frame over transparency, using spray adhesive. ∎

SOURCES: Die cut from K&Company; tree stamp from Duncan; fixative spray from Krylon.

MATERIALS

- 10-inch-square flat wooden frame with 3¾-inch square mirror
- "Love" stamp die cut
- Black mat board or card stock
- Scrap paper
- Printable transparency
- Sandpaper
- Brown spray paint
- Workable fixative spray
- Acrylic sealer
- Tree rubber stamp
- Brown pigment ink pad
- Gold leafing pen
- Stencil brush
- Craft knife
- Adhesive foam squares
- Spray adhesive
- Computer (optional)
- Computer font (optional)

Architectural Accents

DESIGN BY MARY AYRES

Honor your dad this Father's Day with a gift that pays tribute to all his wonderful qualities.

MATERIALS

8 x 10-inch artist's canvas
Printed papers: architecture
   images, stripes
Card stock: concrete, black
Artist's canvas for printer
   (optional)
Black-and-white photo
Alphabet rubber stamps
Domed white typewriter-key
   alphabet stickers
Ink pads: black, brown
Craft paints: dark brown,
   black, cool neutral,
   metallic gold
Black gel stain
Crackle medium
Sealer
Hemp cord
Gold pearl cotton
2¼ x 7-inch brass
   doorknob plate
2 (1-inch) brass hinges
4 (1-inch) ring hangers
Brass picture hanger with nail
Brass charms: key, heart
Gold brads: 12 mini,
   4 regular
Sandpaper
Paintbrushes
Dry sponge
Circle punches: ¹⁄₁₆-inch,
   ½-inch
Hammer
Paper towels
½-inch adhesive
   foam squares
Paper glue
Computer with photo printer
   and scanner (optional)
Computer font (optional)

Project note: Adhere all pieces using scrapbook adhesive unless instructed otherwise.

Mix one part dark brown paint with two parts water; brush onto top and sides of artist's canvas, holding canvas vertically so mixture will be heavier across bottom. Let dry. **Option:** *Use blow dryer to speed drying.* Repeat as desired.

Sand doorknob plate; brush with sealer. Brush with one or two coats black paint. Brush one heavy coat of crackle medium over paint; let dry thoroughly. Brush one coat of gold paint over crackle medium; cracks will appear as paint dries.

Sand regular brads; attach in holes in doorknob plate. Brush plate with black gel stain; wipe off excess using damp paper towel. Adhere plate in bottom left corner of canvas using adhesive foam squares.

From architecture printed paper, cut arch image and 4½ x 5-inch rectangle. Using dry sponge, rub edges with brown ink. Center arch over doorknob plate; adhere. Adhere rectangle in bottom right corner of canvas, wrapping ½ inch of rectangle over edge. Lightly sand edges of canvas and paper.

Use computer to generate, or hand-print, "The Best" on striped paper. Cut 1½ x 1¼-inch rectangle around words; using dry sponge, rub edges with brown ink. Cut 1¾ x 1½-inch rectangle from black card stock. Punch ½-inch circle from center bottom of rectangles; adhere both in center of doorknob plate.

Using typewriter stickers, alphabet stamps and black ink pad, stamp "my dad" on 2¾ x ⅝-inch rectangle concrete card stock, using stickers for first letter in each word. Using dry sponge, rub edges with brown ink; glue rectangle onto arch.

Cut four 4¼ x ⅝-inch strips concrete card stock. Cut four 1 x ⅝-inch strips from black card stock; adhere one to left side of each concrete strip. Sand ring hangers. Brush with black gel stain; wipe off excess using damp paper towel. Punch ¹⁄₁₆-inch holes in card stock where rings will be placed; attach mini brads in holes. Adhere square end of ring hanger to left side of black rectangle; repeat with remaining hangers and rectangles.

Using typewriter stickers, alphabet stamps and black ink pad, stamp descriptive words on concrete rectangles, using stickers for first letter in each word. Trim rectangles; using dry sponge, rub edges with brown ink. Adhere assembled words down right side of doorknob plate.

Cut 3⅜ x 4-inch rectangle black card stock; cut out center, leaving ¼-inch-wide frame. Use computer to scan and print wallet-size photo on back of canvas printer paper. **Option:** *Have photo printed at photography studio.* Trim photo to fit behind frame; adhere.

Sand hinges. Brush with black gel stain; wipe off excess using damp paper towel. Adhere hinges to sides of frame and at center of photo. Punch ¹⁄₁₆-inch holes through frame where hinges will be attached; attach hinges using mini brads. Adhere assembled frame in upper right corner of canvas.

Sand picture hanger and charms. Brush with black gel stain; wipe off excess using damp paper towel. Dry-brush key charm with cool neutral paint. Hammer nail and picture hanger at center top of canvas. String charms onto hemp cord and pearl cotton; tie to picture hanger. ■

SOURCES: Printed papers and typewriter key stickers from K&Company; rubber stamps from Delta/Rubber Stampede.

MATERIALS

Unfinished bird feeder
Printed paper
Fabric "Father" quotation
"Father" die-cut sticker
¼- to ⅜-inch rub-on
   transfers: letters, numerals
Sepia ink pad
Waterproof wood finish
Sandpaper
Soft cloth
Foam brush
Waterproof decoupage
   medium
Double-sided adhesive
   sheets

Tweets for Dad

DESIGN BY KATHLEEN PANEITZ

While this bird feeder is finished to use outdoors, you may want to replace the birdseed with candy for Dad!

Sand bird feeder. Apply decoupage medium; wipe off after 5 minutes. Apply another coat if desired.

Adhere printed paper to sides of bird feeder using double-sided adhesive sheets. Rub edges of fabric quotation on ink pad; adhere quotation to one side of bird feeder. Adhere sticker to other side. On remaining sides, apply rub-on transfers to spell "FATHER'S DAY" and the year.

Coat bird feeder with wood finish. ∎

SOURCES: Printed paper and fabric quotation from Kopp Designs; sticker from Making Memories; rub-on transfers from Autumn Leaves; decoupage medium from Duncan.

Photo Surprise Frame

DESIGN BY NICOLE JACKSON

Place favorite photos in an accordion arrangement so that they can be changed on a whim. Each day a new face takes center stage!

For each photo smaller than 3¾ inches square, stamp background design onto a card stock square using ink pad or paint. Attach card-stock squares accordion-style using flip fasteners.

Adhere photos to card-stock squares. Embellish photos and/or card-stock margins as desired using rub-on transfers. Close accordion; wrap ribbon around it and knot.

Place accordion in frame. Apply rub-on transfers to glass to spell "happy father's day" or other message. **Option:** *Sand back of frame so that it is easy to open and remove photos.* ■

SOURCES: Shadow frame from EK Success; rubber stamp from Hero Arts; rub-on transfers from Making Memories and The C-Thru Ruler Co.; fasteners from Destination Stickers & Stamps Inc.

MATERIALS
4-inch-square shadowbox frame
Photos: 1 (3¾ inches square), and 3 others no larger than 3¾ inches square
4 (3¾-inch) squares card stock
Rub-on transfers
Background rubber stamp
Paint or ink pad
Flip fasteners
Ribbon
Sandpaper (optional)
Double-sided tape

Do-Dad Paint Can

DESIGN BY SHERRY WRIGHT

Present Dad with a gift of small tools and a gift card to his favorite hardware store wrapped up in this fun and masculine package.

MATERIALS

Clean, new paint can with lid
Printed papers: stripes, swirls
Alphabet rub-on transfers
Cream acrylic paint
Foam alphabet stamps
Rubber stamps: leaf,
    alphabet
Solvent ink pads:
    brown, black
Mailbox alphabet tiles
1-inch round alphabet
    stickers
Paper "my dad" image
1-inch metal "D" stencil
Metal key charm
Hammer
1½-inch bottle caps
½-inch alphabet bottle caps
2-inch metal washer
Ribbons
Double-sided adhesive tape
Craft cement
Adhesive foam squares

Cut two 12 x 16-inch pieces striped paper; adhere around bottom of paint can using double-sided adhesive. Cut two 12 x 3½-inch strips of swirl paper; test-fit around top of can and cut notches to accommodate handle; adhere. Cut a circle of swirl paper to fit in center of lid; adhere. Adhere ribbon around can, covering seam between papers.

On front of can, spell "DO" using mailbox alphabet tiles. Stamp "DAD" using foam stamps and cream acrylic paint. Flatten 1½-inch bottle cap; affix "D" sticker in center and adhere over ribbon ends using craft cement.

On lid, adhere "my dad" image using adhesive foam squares. Flatten 1½-inch bottle cap; affix "L" sticker in center; follow with alphabet bottle caps to complete the word "love." Add "U" mailbox tile. Stamp leaves over washer using brown ink; stamp "DAD" over leaves using black ink. Knot metal "D" stencil and key onto ends of ribbon; knot ribbons through washer and adhere washer to lid. Knot lengths of ribbon around handle. ■

SOURCES: Alphabet and foam stamps from Making Memories; bottle caps from Li'l Davis Designs; stencil from Scrapworks; image from me & my BIG ideas; stamps from Duncan; solvent ink from Tsukineko Inc.

All-American Clipboard

DESIGN BY SUSAN HUBER

While you can't actually write on it, this altered clipboard makes a great place to hang notes and reminders to your family.

Project note: Adhere pieces using craft adhesive unless instructed otherwise.

Paint clipboard with one or two coats gesso, until completely covered.

Cut 6½-inch square blue card stock and 2-inch-wide strips red card stock for stripes. "Distress" card stock using sandpaper; adhere to clipboard.

Stamp "CELEBRATE" up left side using brick red ink. Adhere rub-on transfers to card stock as desired.

Ink die-cut stars with light beige ink; adhere to bottom red stripe. Embellish stickers using brads, decorative fibers, etc. Adhere stickers to clipboard using adhesive foam tape. Adhere twill ribbon down white stripes.

Thread waxed red thread through holes in star buttons; adhere buttons and rhinestone stars to clipboard.

Embellish acrylic pieces as desired; adhere to clipboard, or suspend from brad on waxed thread.

Mount sticker on card stock; adhere to clip on clipboard. Knot two complementary fibers through hole in clip. ■

SOURCES: Star die cuts from QuicKutz Inc., rubber stamps, rub-on transfers and ribbon from Making Memories; distress ink from Ranger Industries; stickers from Karen Foster Design; mini brads from Queen & Co.; cork stars from LazerLetterz; rhinestone stars from Westrim; wax-coated thread from Scrapworks.

MATERIALS

Standard clipboard
Card stock: red, blue
White die-cut stars
2³⁄₈-inch alphabet rubber stamps
Distress inks: light beige, brick red
Gesso
Patriotic stickers
Patriotic rub-on transfers
Mini brads: red round, blue square
Cork stars
Acrylic star buttons
Acrylic "July 4th" panel and frame
Faux rhinestone stars
Waxed red thread
Fibers: gold cord, red, white and blue ribbon, string, cord
⁷⁄₈-inch-wide red, white and blue twill ribbon
Paintbrush
Sandpaper
Adhesive foam tape
Craft adhesive

My Hero

DESIGN BY MARY AYRES

MATERIALS

6 x 9-inch artist's canvas
Card stock: metallic gold, light tan
Printed papers: red with U.S. Constitution, white with red dots, tan with "freedom" words, blue
2¾ x 1⅜-inch tea-dyed tag
Vintage photo
Dark blue ink pad
3½ x 5¾ burgundy banner with tassel
2 gold mini brads
3 (⅝-inch) gold buttons
4 gold photo corners
Small dry sponge
1/16-inch circle punch
Sandpaper
Paper glue
Computer (optional)
Computer font (optional)

Give a vintage photo of a veteran the place of honor in your home!

Cut strips from printed papers: 7 x 4½ inches red, 7 x 3 inches white polka-dot, 7 x 1½ inches tan, and 7 x 2½ inches blue. Tear along top edges of all pieces except red. Using dry sponge, rub torn edges with dark blue ink.

Adhere strips across canvas from top down, overlapping strips and wrapping edges over sides of canvas. **Option:** *Score paper first where it will be folded for a crisp look.* Adhere red strip first, then white polka-dot, tan and blue. Trim corners as needed before adhering edges. Lightly sand papers on top and edges.

Cut metallic gold card stock ⅛ inch larger all around than tea-dyed tag; adhere tag in center. Use computer to generate, or hand-print, "Hero" on tan card stock. Cut out, positioning word in center of 1¾ x ¾-inch rectangle; use dry sponge to rub edges with dark blue ink. Adhere rectangle in center of tag.

Punch 1/16-inch holes in ends of "Hero" rectangle; mount mini brads in holes. Tie ends of tag cord in a bow. Adhere assembled tag in bottom left corner of canvas. Arrange and adhere buttons to tag.

Adhere banner to upper right corner of canvas. Place gold corners on photo; center and adhere photo to banner. ■

SOURCES: Printed papers and tag from Rusty Pickle; blue printed paper from Keeping Memories Alive; tassel banner from EK Success.

Patriotic Spheres

DESIGN BY LORINE MASON

While these globes have a distinct flavor of Americana, you can substitute handmade paper and metallic creams to produce a sophisticated look.

MATERIALS
4-inch plastic foam ball
Americana-theme
    printed paper
Raw sienna craft paint
Gloss finish
1½ yards waxed linen thread
    to complement/contrast
    with paper
Paintbrush
Soft cloth
Water-based super glue

Tear paper into uneven pieces. Coat backs of pieces with glue; adhere to plastic foam ball, overlapping edges to cover completely. Let dry.

Mix one part paint with two parts water. Brush diluted paint onto ball; wipe with a soft cloth, leaving paint in crevices. Let dry.

Paint ball with two coats gloss finish.

Tie loop in end of thread. Wrap thread around ball and thread end through loop; pull taut. Continue wrapping ball, dividing it into eight segments. Knot thread; trim ends. ■

SOURCE: STYROFOAM® brand plastic foam balls from Dow Chemical Co.

Independence Day Tray

DESIGN BY LINDA BEESON

MATERIALS
Wooden tray
Red spray paint
Red, white and blue
    printed papers: stars, red
    handwriting
Card stock: red, blue
    (optional)
Patriotic stickers
Word "label" stickers
Word rub-on transfers:
    "celebrate," "apple pie"
Red, white and blue ribbons
    (optional)
Paintbrush
Circle punch (optional)
Decoupage medium

Serve a portion of all-American fun on this tray covered with decoupaged stars and patriotic phrases!

Project note: Use decoupage medium to adhere all elements.

Spray tray with red paint. Cut star printed paper to fit in bottom of tray; adhere. Cut ¾-inch-wide strips of red printed paper to fit around perimeter of bottom of tray; tear strips along inner edges. Adhere strips in bottom of tray. Cut strips of red printed paper to fit along top inside edges of tray; adhere.

Adhere patriotic stickers and rub-on transfer words in bottom of tray. Paint tray with two or three coats of decoupage medium.

OPTIONAL TAG
Adhere red card stock to blue card stock; cut out tag shape, leaving a blue border. Punch hole in top of tag; reinforce hole with a circle cut from printed paper or a round sticker if desired.

Embellish tag with star printed paper and stickers. Coat tag with decoupage medium. Thread ribbons through hole. ■

SOURCES: Printed papers from 7 gypsies and Daisy D's Paper Co., patriotic stickers from Karen Foster Design; label stickers from EK Success; rub-on transfers from Making Memories.

Fourth of July CD

DESIGN BY SHERRY WRIGHT

Create a festive decoration for your doors or windows! Display several to show off your American spirit!

Project note: *Adhere pieces using adhesive dots unless instructed otherwise.*

Sand CD so that paper glue will adhere. Trace around CD twice onto printed paper; cut out. Adhere one circle to front of CD; set second circle aside.

Adhere fabric tag to CD. Color "4" stencil with red ink pad. Cut 3-inch pieces of red, white and blue ribbons; fold in half and staple along left edge of stencil. Adhere stencil to left edge of fabric tag. Adhere stickers at top of CD and on fabric tag.

Transfer rub-on transfers to fabric tag to add "th" after the "4" stencil; transfer "JULY" to top of CD. Adhere bottle cap to CD and fabric tag at upper right corner of tag.

Adhere half of vellum tag between bottom edge of fabric tag and CD. Mount star brad through vellum. Punch ⅛-inch hole in vellum; thread red gingham ribbon through hole. Punch hole near top of remaining bottle caps using hammer and nail; thread bottle caps onto ribbon ends.

Glue ends of ⅜-inch-wide red ribbon to back of CD for hanger; adhere remaining circle of printed paper to back of CD using paper glue. Knot blue gingham and solid white ribbons around hanger. ∎

SOURCES: Printed paper from Provo Craft; stencil, fabric tag and rub-on transfers from Making Memories; bottle caps from Li'l Davis Designs.

MATERIALS

Blank CD
Printed paper
 "4" numeral stencil
Red ink pad
4½ x 3-inch blue denim
    fabric tag
Alphabet rub-on transfers
3 Fourth of July bottle caps
1¾-inch round vellum tag
    with red rim
Silver star brad
Stickers: Statue of Liberty,
    Liberty bell
Ribbon: ⅜-inch-wide red;
    ¼-inch-wide solid white,
    red gingham, blue gingham
Fine-grit sandpaper
Stapler and staples
⅛-inch circle punch
Hammer and small nail
Paper glue
Adhesive dots

Patriotic Box

DESIGN BY KATHLEEN PANEITZ

MATERIALS

Round papier-mâché box
    with lid
Red, white and blue plaid
    printed paper
Cream card stock
Star rubber stamp
Craft paints: red, navy,
    off-white
Light beige distress ink pad
2 red eyelets and eyelet-
    setting tool
String
Paintbrushes
Circle punch
Double-sided adhesive sheet

This red, white and blue storage box will be right at home in a warm, country-style room.

Project note: Adhere all pieces using pieces cut from double-sided adhesive sheet.

Paint exterior of lid navy; paint exterior of box red. Using off-white paint as ink, stamp stars on lid, spacing them evenly around edge.

Piece together two 1⅜-inch-wide strips printed paper, matching plaids, to make a strip long enough to go around box, less ¾ inch. Cut two ½ x 1⅜-inch rectangles cream card stock; adhere over ends of printed strip. Punch holes through strip in center of card-stock rectangles; set eyelets in holes.

Adhere printed paper strip around box. Thread string through eyelets; tie in a bow. ■

SOURCES: Printed paper from Pixie Press; rubber stamp from Duncan; distress ink from Ranger Industries.

U.S.A. Wall Decor

DESIGN BY SUSAN STRINGFELLOW

Premade letters covered with patriotic-themed papers and paints make a perfect wall accent for your Fourth of July gatherings!

Paint "U" blue, "S" white and "A" dark red. Brush edges of "U" lightly with white. Cover fronts of letters with matching colors of printed paper, adhering paper with paper glaze. Rub front edges of letters with light brown ink pad.

Arrange letters facedown with edges touching; adhere where edges touch using craft cement. Adhere wooden craft stick across backs of letters using craft cement.

Tie ribbons and rickrack around letters. Mount white mini brad through hole in "HOPE" tag; adhere charm to "U" using craft cement. Fill star charm with paper glaze; sprinkle with ultrafine glitter. Adhere charm to "S" using craft cement. Poke dark red mini brad through center of silk flower; adhere flower to "A" using craft cement.

Using black solvent ink pad, stamp stars on lower edges of "U," "S" and left leg of "A"; stamp "FREEDOM" on bottom right leg of "A." ∎

SOURCES: Wooden letters from Provo Craft; printed papers from Making Memories, Flair and Pressed Petals; star stamp from Stampin' Up!; tag from Colorbök; charm from Making Memories; solvent ink from Tsukineko Inc.; paper glaze from JudiKins.

MATERIALS

6-inch wooden letters to spell "USA"

Printed paper: blue and red fabric weaves, white patriotic

Craft paints: dark red, white, blue

Rubber stamps: star, alphabet

Light brown ink pad

Black solvent ink pad

Ultrafine glitter

Mini brads: white, dark red

Star charm

Metal "HOPE" tag

Blue silk flower

Ribbons: red, blue

White rickrack

Paintbrushes

Wooden craft stick

Heavy-duty craft cement or wood glue

Paper glaze

A Puzzling Surprise

DESIGN BY SUSAN STRINGFELLOW

This box of blocks puts a new twist on scrapbooking! Photocopied scrapbook pages are decoupaged onto wooden blocks to create six different puzzles!

Project note: Adhere all elements using decoupage medium unless instructed otherwise instructed.

BLOCKS

Place blocks in box. Make sure there will be sufficient room for blocks in box when they are covered on all sides with paper or card stock. Sand blocks as needed to ease fit.

Create six square layouts using photos, papers, stickers and embellishments as desired. Arrange all blocks in a square; measure square's dimensions, then scan and print layouts to match this measurement—7⅜ inches square, in this case.

One by one, cut layouts into squares to fit on sides of blocks; adhere squares to blocks. Repeat until all layouts have been cut out and all pieces adhered to blocks.

Rub edges of blocks with black ink pad. Apply two coats varnish to each block.

BOX

Remove clasp. Paint box black inside and out. Apply crackle medium to exterior; let dry. Apply orange paint over crackle medium. Cracks will appear; let dry.

Rub edges of a 5½ x 4¾-inch piece of printed paper with black ink pad; adhere in upper left corner of box lid. Rub edges of a 12 x 1¼-inch strip of striped paper with black ink pad; center and adhere across lid near bottom edge, wrapping ends down sides and onto bottom of box. Rub top edges of box with black ink pad. Use craft knife to slice through paper where lid and box bottom meet.

Use computer to generate, or hand-print, "Halloween" *in reverse* on wrong side of lime green card stock; cut out using craft knife. Rub letters with black ink pad; adhere along left edge of lid.

Rub edges of kitty image using black ink pad; mount on black card stock. Adhere to lid.

Paint lid and sides with one coat varnish. Reattach clasp.

Lightly brush cork "Boo!" with lime paint; brush varnish across top. Wrap 3-inch lengths of ribbon around left edge of "B"; secure ribbons with mini brads. Adhere cork "Boo!" to lid.

Cut printed paper to fit inside lid; adhere. Rub edges of 3-inch and 2-inch squares of printed paper with black ink pad; adhere inside box lid. Stamp with pumpkin image using black ink. Paint interior of box with one coat varnish. ■

SOURCES: Box of Blocks from The Little Scrapbook Store; printed papers and acrylic tiles from KI Memories; cork "Boo!" from LazerLetterz; Halloween kitty image from Altered Pages; solvent ink from Tsukineko Inc.; crackle medium, paints and decoupage medium from Plaid.

MATERIALS
Wooden box of blocks
Printed papers
Halloween kitty image
Card stock: lime, black
Stickers
Acrylic tiles
Cork letters to spell "Boo!"
Craft paints: black, orange, lime
Crackle medium
Indoor/outdoor varnish
Black solvent ink pad
Mini brads: lime, black
Ribbons
Sandpaper (optional)
Paintbrush
Craft knife
Color photocopier
Decoupage medium
Computer (optional)
Computer font (optional)

Witch's Hat Centerpiece

DESIGN BY MARY AYRES

Dress up your home for Halloween with a unique table decoration. Paper-winged bats and webbing spray add to the exceptional design.

Sand funnel; brush with sealer. Paint plate and funnel black (including interior at tip). Spray funnel and bottom of plate with webbing spray. Glue funnel to back of plate.

For buckle, cut 2½ x 3-inch rectangle gold card stock; round corners and cut rectangle from center. Using dry sponge, rub edges with brown ink.

Print boy-with-pumpkins image from CD-ROM onto white card stock. **Option:** *Use stickers or images from magazines or greeting cards.* Cut out; use dry sponge to ink edges. Adhere image to center of buckle.

Punch ⅛-inch hole in each side of buckle; mount eyelets in holes. Thread hemp cord through eyelets. Adhere buckle to hat; tie ends of cord together in back.

For bats, paint clothespins lavender; dry-brush with orange. Using pattern provided, cut two sets of bat wings from rawhide-texture paper. Accordion-fold sides of wings.

Leaving 3-inch tail at head (closed end), wrap wire several times around clothespin; leave long tail at other end to wrap around funnel. Adhere clothespin in center of paper wings. Repeat to make second bat. Coil short wire ends around pencil; wrap long wire tails around tip of hat.

Print "Halloween Joys" from CD-ROM onto white card stock. **Option:** *Use computer to generate, or hand-print, words.* Cut out; use dry sponge to ink edges. Punch ⅛-inch hole in left side; set eyelet in hole. Thread hemp cord through eyelet; wrap cord around top of hat several times and knot ends. Wrap fall foliage around hat brim. ∎

SOURCES: Textured paper from Provo Craft; Halloween images CD-ROM from The Vintage Workshop; webbing spray from Krylon; hemp cord and wire from Toner Plastic.

DIAGRAM ON PAGE 162

MATERIALS

- 10½-inch papier-mâché plate
- 1-quart galvanized funnel
- Card stock: white, metallic gold
- Rawhide-texture paper
- Halloween images from CD-ROM
- Brown ink pad
- Craft paints: black, lavender, orange
- Gold webbing spray
- 3 (⅛-inch) antique eyelets and eyelet-setting tool
- 2 mini spring clothespins
- Purple hemp cord
- Black 22-gauge wire
- Artificial fall foliage
- Sealer
- Sandpaper
- Paintbrushes
- Small dry sponge
- Corner rounder
- ⅛-inch circle punch
- Craft glue
- Computer (optional)
- Computer font (optional)

Halloween Bracelet

DESIGN BY SUSAN STRINGFELLOW

Altered bottle caps and spooky papers combine to make a fun and festive Halloween fashion accessory!

MATERIALS

5 bottle caps
Striped printed paper
Halloween bottle
    cap stickers
Decorative flat buttons:
    kitty, ghost
3/8-inch-wide gingham
    check ribbons: lime/
    yellow, orange/yellow
Coat hook-and-eye closure
Rubber mallet
Hammer and small nail
1-inch circle punch
    (optional)
Large-eye needle
Paper glaze

Project note: *Adhere all pieces using paper glaze.*

Flatten bottle caps using rubber mallet. Punch two holes in each bottle cap near edges on opposite sides using hammer and nail.

Adhere Halloween stickers inside three bottle caps. Punch or cut two 1-inch circles from striped paper; adhere inside remaining bottle caps. Center and adhere ghost and kitty buttons in these bottle caps.

String bottle caps together using 2½-inch lengths of ribbon, alternating ribbon colors and bottle caps with stickers and buttons. Knot hook and eye onto ends of bracelet. ■

SOURCES: Bottle caps and stickers from Design Originals; printed paper from KI Memories; buttons from Doodlebug Designs; paper glaze from JudiKins.

Trick or Treat Candle

DESIGN BY SUSAN STRINGFELLOW

This friendly black cat sits perched and ready to welcome little ghosts and goblins to your home.

Project note: *Pierce candle with thin, sharp scissors to make it easier to insert brads.*

Center 8¼ x 2¼-inch strip black card stock over 8¼ x 3¼-inch strip adhesive mesh; tear an 8¼ x 1¼-inch strip from orange fabric and center over card stock. Wrap strips around candle, securing overlapped ends on back.

Using black ink, stamp kitty onto white card stock; cut out. Rub edges with orange and black ink pads. Adhere stamped image on black card stock; cut out, leaving narrow border.

Punch three ⅛-inch holes in lower right corner; knot 2-inch lengths of gold and black rickrack through holes. Twist 4 x 1-inch strip black adhesive mesh in center; adhere to fabric strip on front of candle. Using a thin, sharp scissors, pierce two holes in left edge of kitty panel. Attach panel to candle using orange brads, overlapping twist in mesh. Rub heads of brads with black ink pad.

Knot two 3-inch pieces gold and black rickrack around black mini brad; attach to candle near top left corner of kitty panel. ■

SOURCES: Stamp from Close To My Heart; mesh from Magenta; solvent ink from Tsukineko Inc.

MATERIALS
3-inch-diameter x 6-inch Halloween pillar candle
Card stock: black, white textured
Black adhesive mesh
Kitty rubber stamp
Black solvent ink pad
Orange ink pad
Brads: 2 orange, 1 mini black
Orange fabric
Rickrack: gold, black
⅛-inch circle punch
Thin, sharp scissors
Glue

Ghostly Greetings

DESIGN BY SUSAN HUBER

Vintage artwork and brightly colored fibers combine to create a fun door hanger to greet your spooky guests.

MATERIALS

Card stock: black, green, rust textured
Vintage Halloween images
Ghost stickers
Cork letters to spell "boo"
Mini brads: green, orange
$3/8$-inch-wide ribbons: lime/yellow, orange/yellow and black/white gingham check; green and gold solid
Black/white gingham ribbon bow
Yellow chalk
Green fibers
Orange rickrack
$1/2$-inch-wide orange twill tape
Black craft wire
Pumpkin die (optional)
$1/8$-inch circle punch
Craft glue
Double-sided tape
Adhesive foam tape

Cut 4⅞ x 7⅞-inch rust card stock; adhere to black card stock using double-sided tape. Trim, leaving very narrow border. Wrap green fiber and orange rickrack across bottom, gluing ends on back. Vertically wrap green fibers around panel near left edge, gluing ends on back. Adhere orange twill tape to right of green fibers, securing ends with green mini brads.

Lightly sand girl-with-pumpkin image; adhere in upper right corner using double-sided tape. Adhere ribbon bow to upper left corner using glue.

Adhere black cat image to rust card stock using double-sided tape; trim, leaving narrow border. Adhere to black card stock; trim, leaving wider border down left edge. Cut two 2-inch pieces of black/white gingham ribbon and one piece of orange/gold. Fold ribbons in half; attach to upper left edge of black card stock using orange and green mini brads. Adhere black cat panel at an angle using foam tape; tuck bottom right corner under rickrack and green fiber.

Adhere larger ghost sticker above black cat image using foam tape. Adhere smaller ghost sticker directly to rust card stock to right of black cat.

Using pumpkin die, cut three pumpkins from rust card stock and tendrils from green. **Option:** *Cut pumpkins and tendrils with scissors.* Chalk edges of pumpkins. Arrange pumpkins near bottom right corner; adhere using foam tape. Adhere tendrils using glue. Adhere cork letters to spell "boo" above larger ghost using glue.

Punch ⅛-inch holes in upper corners; secure ends of coiled wire through holes for hanger. Knot 3-inch pieces of ribbon onto wire, alternating gold, green, orange/gold gingham and black/white gingham; repeat pattern three more times. Trim ribbon ends. ■

SOURCES: Halloween images from Altered Pages; stickers from Karen Foster Design; cork letters from LazerLetterz; mini brads, ribbons and bow from Queen & Co; pumpkin die from QuicKutz Inc.

Tiny Treat Boxes

DESIGNS BY NICOLE JACKSON

These are quick to make and fun to give. Create a bunch to fill with Halloween treats!

Using pattern provided, trace box template onto wrong side of printed paper; cut out. Score along dashed lines; fold to create box, but do not adhere sides.

Lightly mark where slot should be cut for flap, in center of bottom front crease. Lay box flat; cut slot using craft knife.

Embellish box as desired; adhere embellishments using craft adhesive. Refold box; secure sides using double-sided tape.

Fill box with treats; insert tab in slot. ■

SOURCES: Printed papers and tags from KI Memories; rubber stamps from Ma Vinci's Reliquary; rub-on transfers from Making Memories.

PATTERN ON PAGE 170

MATERIALS
7½-inch square of
   printed paper
Rubber stamps (optional)
Ink pad (optional)
Desired embellishments:
   paper tags, rub-on
   transfers, ribbons, etc.
Craft knife
Double-sided tape
Craft adhesive

Halloween Paper Quilt

DESIGN BY MARY AYRES

The time-honored craft of quilting carries over into paper with this whimsical wall quilt. Odds and ends from your craft stash make this a one-of-a-kind creation.

Project note: Adhere all pieces using scrapbook adhesive unless instructed otherwise.

Using dry sponge, rub edges of one sheet gray card stock with purple ink. Using ruler and pencil, divide sheet into nine 4-inch squares. Using sewing machine threaded with black thread, straight-stitch over lines; adhere thread ends on back. Adhere second sheet of gray card stock to back of stitched square.

Cut quilt block motif from each of nine printed papers; rub edges with purple ink. Adhere shapes in squares on card stock with points in corners. Glue buttons to corners of squares.

Using patterns provided, embellish squares, adhering embellishments using scrapbook adhesive:

Top left: Adhere pumpkin image over gauze fabric.

Top center: Using black stain, antique metal bookplates. Use computer to generate, or hand-print, "happy" and "haunting" on card stock; insert in bookplates. Use gold mini brads to adhere bookplates to quilt.

Top right: Adhere copper alphabet letters to spell "BOO" to tea-dyed tag; add eyelet and hemp cord bow.

Center left: Rub edges of zipper with purple ink; tie on key using hemp cord.

Center center: Adhere photo behind slide mount.

Center right: Tear moon from yellow handmade paper; rub edges with gold ink. Adhere cat image.

Bottom left: Rub edges of Victorian "H" with brown ink. Adhere round frame; using yellow pencil, color area inside frame.

Bottom center: Cut star halves from orange handmade paper; rub edges with gold ink. Antique hinge using black stain; adhere over star halves using silver mini brads.

Bottom right: Dry-brush leaf plaque with orange paint; adhere over pinked adhesive splattered net.

Paint dowel gold. Cut four 3½-inch pieces of ribbon; fold each into loop. Glue 1 inch of ribbon ends across top back edge of paper quilt; insert dowel through loops. ■

SOURCES: Halloween images and Victorian "H" from Dover Publications; round frame and copper "BOO" from K&Company; hinge from Magic Scraps; leaf plaque from Making Memories; buttons and zipper from Junkitz; splatter net from Jest Charming Embellishments; scrapbook adhesive from Decorator's Solution.

PATTERNS ON PAGE 162

MATERIALS

- ³/₈-inch-diameter wooden dowel
- 2 (12-inch) squares gray card stock
- Printed papers: 9 assorted designs
- Handmade papers: yellow, orange
- 2½ x 1½-inch tea-dyed tag
- 3½-inch-square walnut watermarks slide mount
- Vintage Halloween images
- Victorian-style "H"
- Photo
- Ink pads: purple, brown, gold
- Black stain
- Craft paints: gold metallic, burnt orange
- 16 flat buttons
- 2 metal bookplates
- Mini brads: 4 gold, 4 silver
- Round copper letters to spell "BOO"
- Gold eyelet and eyelet-setting tool
- 1½-inch gold key
- 1-inch round metal frame
- Silver metal hinge
- 1½ x 1⁷/₈-inch maple leaf plaque
- 4-inch green zipper
- Gauze fabric
- Tan splattered adhesive net
- Black hemp cord
- ³/₈-inch-wide black striped ribbon
- Yellow colored pencil
- Small dry sponge
- Sewing machine with black thread
- ⅛-inch circle punch
- Paintbrushes
- Ruler
- Pinking shears
- Scrapbook adhesive
- Computer (optional)
- Computer fonts (optional)

Candy Corn Halloween Plate

DESIGN BY SANDY ROLLINGER

Use this fun Halloween plate to serve ghostly treats and scary snacks! The design is sealed on the back, so the plate can be gently hand-washed.

MATERIALS
12-inch clear glass plate
Mulberry paper: orange, yellow
White-on-black pin-dot paper
Candy corn photo paper
Permanent gold metallic pen
Spiral paper punch
½-inch soft craft brush
Decoupage medium

Cut individual candy corns from paper. Punch spirals from black pin-dot paper.

Brush center area on back of plate with decoupage medium; press a single candy corn into medium in center of plate, right side against glass. Adhere additional candy corns to back of plate, spacing them 2–3 inches apart. In same fashion, adhere spirals in spaces between candy corns. Let dry completely.

Tear yellow and orange mulberry papers into 2-inch pieces. Adhere pieces of yellow paper over spirals using decoupage medium; let dry. Adhere pieces of orange paper over candy corns using decoupage medium. Let dry, then brush entire back of plate with one more coat of decoupage medium; let dry.

Color edges of plate with permanent gold pen.

Use plate to serve cookies, cakes or candies. Do not immerse plate in water. Wipe off surface using a damp cloth. ■

SOURCES: Printed papers from Die Cuts With A View; decoupage medium from Beacon.

Orange-Peel Autumn

DESIGNS BY LORINE MASON

The surprise ingredient in this project? Orange peel motifs that have been cut with tiny cookie or canapé cutters and dried to form autumn embellishments.

ORANGE PEEL MOTIFS

Cut oak leaves and acorns from orange peel using canapé cutters. Punch hole in each using ⅛-inch circle punch. Let shapes dry overnight.

CANDLE

Tear 1½-inch-wide strip of printed paper long enough to go around candle and overlap 1 inch. Wrap paper around candle; tie in place using waxed thread. Thread orange peel motifs onto ends of thread; knot. Wrap thread ends tightly around skewer to coil; remove skewer.

PLACE CARDS & INVITATIONS

Use computer to generate, or hand-print, party information or guest's names on vellum. If desired, add autumn message:

I walked on paths of crisp dry leaves after, that flamed with color and crackled with laughter.

For *place cards,* cut printed paper 4 x 5 inches; fold in half lengthwise. Center 2 x 3-inch piece of vellum on front. Punch two ¹⁄₁₆-inch holes at opposite corners through both layers; insert thread through holes to attach vellum to paper. Thread orange peel motifs onto ends of thread; knot. Wrap thread ends tightly around skewer to coil; remove skewer.

For *invitations,* cut printed paper 4 x 5½ inches and vellum 3¼ x 4 inches; center vellum over paper. Finish as for place cards. ■

MATERIALS

Orange peels
Candle
Autumn printed paper
Gold vellum
Mini canapé cutters: acorn, oak leaf
Waxed thread: ivory, beige
Skewer
Circle punches: ⅛-inch, ¹⁄₁₆-inch
Computer (optional)
Computer font (optional)

Autumn Wall Canvas

DESIGN BY SUZIE SHINSEKI, COURTESY OF DUNCAN ENTERPRISES

Decoupaged leaves take on a realistic look with strategically placed lines of paint.

MATERIALS

16 x 20-inch artist canvas on frame

8 x 10-inch photo mat with 5 x 7-inch opening

5 x 7-inch photo

¼ x ½-inch basswood strips: 2 (11¾-inch), 2 (14¾-inch)

Tissue paper: orange, yellow, brown, red

Textured mulberry paper: pale yellow, white

Acrylic paints: antique gold, burnt umber

Snow paste

Silk fall leaves with berries

⅝-inch-wide orange ribbon

Matte-finish decoupage medium

Paintbrushes

Palette knife

Quick-setting tacky glue

Pencil

Ruler

Lightly pencil 11 x 15-inch rectangle in center of canvas. Using palette knife, swirl snow paste over canvas outside rectangle to give it texture.

Tear mulberry papers into strips; tear some pieces from yellow tissue. Brush decoupage medium over center rectangle. Lay yellow tissue strips randomly across rectangle. Brush with another layer of decoupage medium; lay on pale yellow and white mulberry strips until rectangle is covered.

Tear orange tissue into rough leaf shapes. Randomly lay leaves over center rectangle; brush with decoupage medium. Lay on more strips of white and pale yellow mulberry paper to soften the bright orange color.

Thin a little antique gold paint with water. Use your fingertips to flick mixture over decoupaged area. Using liner brush dipped in undiluted gold paint, loosely brush leaves to suggest stems and veins.

Tear irregular pieces from orange, brown, red and yellow tissue and white mulberry paper. Decoupage onto outer frame area of canvas; let dry. Dip flat brush into undiluted gold paint; brush lightly over outer, texturized area of canvas.

Paint basswood strips burnt umber; using quick-setting tacky glue, adhere strips around center rectangle. Paint photo mat burnt umber; when dry, flick with thinned gold paint. Brush a ¼-inch border of undiluted gold paint around opening in mat; let dry. Adhere photo behind mat; adhere mat in center of canvas.

Adhere orange ribbon around edges of canvas. Cut ribbon for hanger; nail or staple ends to back of canvas frame. Tie ribbon in a bow at top of hanger, adding fall leaves and berries. ■

SOURCE: Snow paste and decoupage medium from Duncan.

Be Thankful Candle

DESIGN BY SHERRY WRIGHT

Place this candle on a bedside table to help you focus during times of meditation.

MATERIALS

Candle

3 candle wicks with "stick-ums"

¼ of a block of scented wax

Wick-holding sticks

Aluminum melting/pouring pitcher

Saucepan

Glass wax thermometer

Tin

4-inch-diameter round candle tin

Printed papers

Stickers

Silk fall leaves

³/₈-inch-wide sheer beige/bronze ribbon

Adhesive dots

CANDLE

Apply wick "stick-ums" for three wicks inside bottom of tin. Attach wicks, using wick-holding stick to hold them upright. Break wax into small pieces; place in aluminum melting/pouring pitcher.

Add 2 inches of water to saucepan; bring to medium boil. Set pitcher of wax in pan; melt wax, stirring it occasionally and monitoring temperature. When wax temperature reaches 175 degrees Farenheit, pour it slowly into tin, keeping wicks upright and filling tin to about ½ inch from top; reserve a small amount of wax for retopping, as candle will shrink slightly as it cools.

Let tin sit undisturbed for 12 hours. Remelt reserved wax; retop candle. Let dry undisturbed for 2 hours. Remove wick-holding stick; trim wicks to ½ inch.

TIN

Cut strip of printed paper long enough to cover side of tin; adhere around tin, overlapping ends on front. Adhere sticker over paper where it overlaps.

Trace around lid onto printed paper; cut out and trim to fit in center of lid. Adhere paper to lid. Cut ribbon to fit around edge of lid; adhere, overlapping ribbon ends where leaves will overhang lid. Embellish lid with stickers and silk leaves. ■

SOURCE: Printed papers and stickers from SEI.

Gratitude Journal

DESIGN BY KATHLEEN PANEITZ

Use this journal throughout the year to remember what you're thankful for. At Thanksgiving, share your entries with family and friends.

Project Note: *Adhere pieces using double-sided adhesive sheets unless instructed otherwise.*

Remove spine from journal. Cut printed paper ½ inch larger on all sides than covers; adhere paper to covers. Score excess paper along edges; trim corners. Fold excess to inside of covers and secure using ¼-inch double-sided tape.

Cut cream textured card stock slightly smaller than covers; ink edges with sepia ink; adhere inside covers. Repunch holes in covers for spine; reassemble journal.

Mat photo on orange card stock; trim, leaving narrow border. Adhere to cover. Transfer "gratitude" along top of cover using rub-on transfers; add "journal" across bottom using typewriter key stickers. Use computer to print definitions onto cream card stock. **Option:** *Hand-write or type definitions on card stock.* Trim definitions; rub edges with sepia ink pad. Adhere definitions to cover. Tie raffia in a bow around cover. ∎

SOURCES: Printed paper from Daisy D's Paper Co.; rub-on transfers from Autumn Leaves; stickers from K&Company.

MATERIALS

Wire-bound journal
Thanksgiving printed paper
Textured card stock: dark orange, cream
Thanksgiving photo or image
Rub-on alphabet transfers
Black typewriter key stickers
"Blessed" and "abundance" definitions
Raffia
Sepia ink pad
¼-inch circle punch
Double-sided adhesive sheets
¼-inch-wide double-sided tape
Computer (optional)
Computer font (optional)

Harvest-Time Candle

DESIGN BY SHERRY WRIGHT

Use this altered can on its own as a table accent or place it in the center of an autumn candle ring for a buffet centerpiece.

MATERIALS

Candle

Candle wick with "stick-um"

¼ of a block of pumpkin-
spice scented wax

Wick-holding sticks

Aluminum melting/pouring
pitcher

Saucepan

Glass wax thermometer

Can

Clean, new quart paint can

Printed papers

Paper "Giving Thanks" tag

½ x 1⅞-inch metal leaf
plaque

1-inch metal slide buckle

1 x 1⅝-inch mailbox
letter "T"

"Harvest Time" fabric label

⅜-inch-wide beige/bronze
jacquard ribbon

Adhesive dots

CANDLE

Apply wick "stick-um" for wick in bottom of can. Attach wick, using wick-holding stick to hold it upright. Break wax into small pieces; place in aluminum melting/pouring pitcher.

Add 2 inches of water to saucepan; bring to medium boil. Set pitcher of wax in pan; melt wax, stirring it occasionally and monitoring temperature. When wax temperature reaches 175 degrees Farenheit, pour it slowly into tin, keeping wick upright and filling tin to about ½ inch from top; reserve a small amount of wax for retopping, as candle will shrink slightly as it cools.

Let tin sit undisturbed for 12 hours. Remelt reserved wax; retop candle. Let dry undisturbed for 2 hours. Remove wick-holding stick; trim wick to ½ inch.

TIN

Cut printed paper to cover side of can, piecing paper together as needed. Adhere paper around tin, positioning overlap on back.

Trace around lid onto printed paper; cut out and trim to fit in center of lid. Adhere paper to lid.

Cut ribbon to fit around can; slide buckle onto ribbon and adhere, overlapping ribbon ends on back of can. Embellish can with "Harvest Time" fabric label and mailbox "T."

Knot one end of an 8-inch piece of ribbon; knot paper "Giving Thanks" tag on other end. Adhere knotted end of ribbon across top of lid so that paper tag dangles down side of can; adhere metal leaf plaque to center of can lid over ribbon. ■

SOURCES: Printed papers from Imagination Project Inc./Gin-X; buckle and paper tag from EK Success; leaf plaque, buckle and mailbox letter from Making Memories; fabric label from me & my BIG ideas.

Autumn Leaf Basket

DESIGN BY SANDY ROLLINGER

Embossing powder creates realistic textures on air-dry clay leaves. Use them as shown for basket embellishments, or create matching napkin rings by wiring the leaves to coiled wire bases.

MATERIALS
Woven square basket
White air-dry clay
Large maple leaf rubber
    stamp
Embossing ink: orange,
    yellow
Clear embossing powder
Copper acrylic paint
3 large beige/tan buttons
Burlap
Fibers: green, brown
Cornstarch
Protective surface or cutting
    board
Brayer or rolling pin
Magazine
Paintbrush
Soft cloth
Craft knife
Embossing heat tool
Permanent adhesive
Craft cement

Using rolling pin or brayer, roll clay ⅛ inch thick on protective surface. Dust rubber stamp with cornstarch; stamp two leaves on rolled clay, making deep impressions. Cut out leaves using craft knife. Let dry for at least 4 hours, turning leaves occasionally to keep them from curling too much. During the last hour or so, lay a magazine on top of the leaves to keep them flat.

Randomly apply yellow and orange embossing ink to leaves; sprinkle with embossing powder and emboss. When cool, brush copper paint over entire surface of each leaf. Wipe off most of the paint using a dampened soft cloth, leaving most of the color on the edges and in crevices.

Cut 1½-inch-wide strip of burlap long enough to go around basket; remove two or three threads from each long edge for fringe. Adhere strip around top of basket using permanent adhesive. Adhere brown and green fibers around basket over burlap, knotting ends and leaving ends dangling at center front.

Adhere leaves to front of basket and adhere buttons over top of knot using craft cement. ■

SOURCES: Air-dry clay from Creative Paperclay Co.; paint from Jacquard Products; permanent fabric adhesive and craft cement from Beacon.

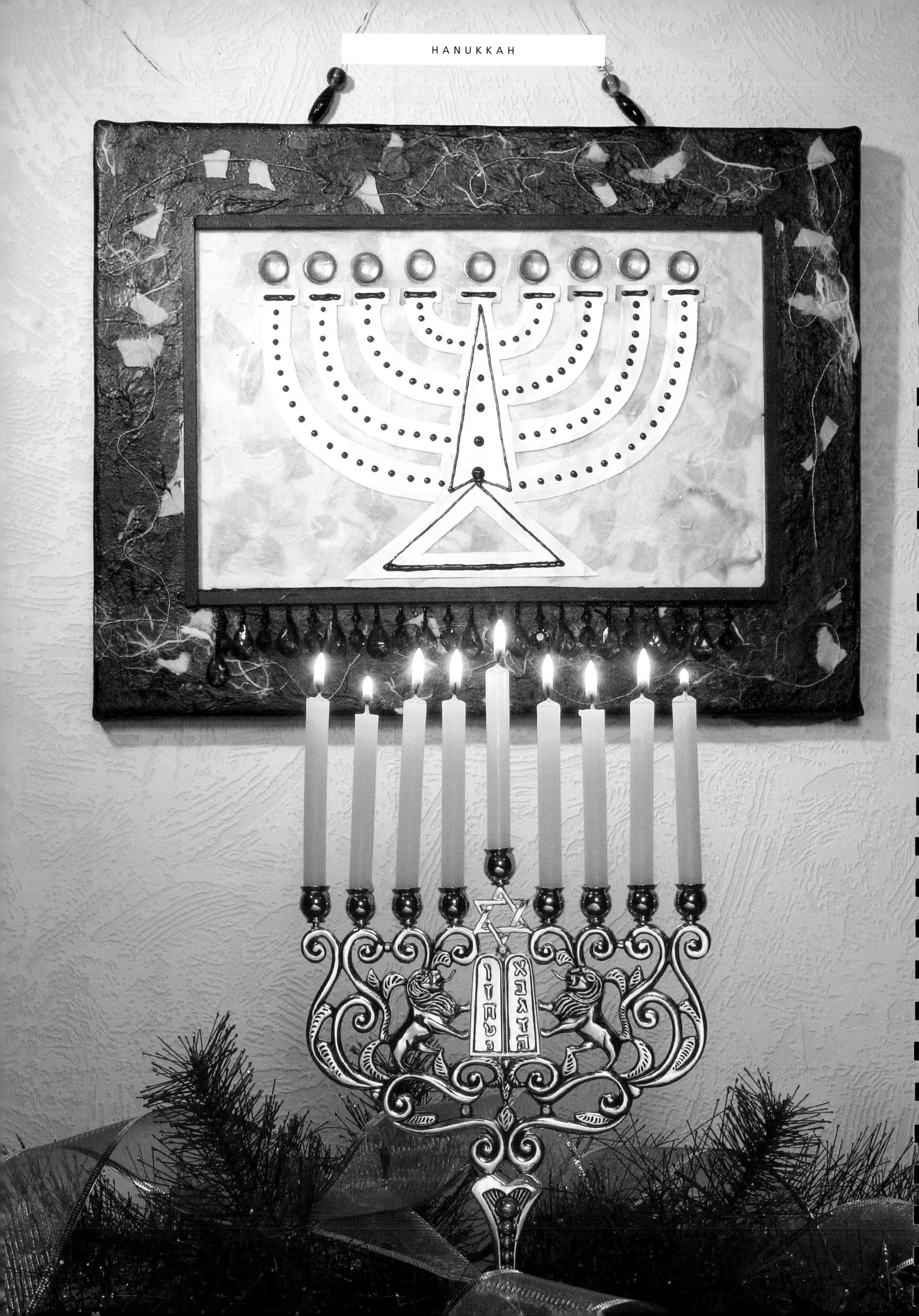

Hanukkah Wall Canvas

DESIGN BY SUZIE SHINSEKI, COURTESY OF DUNCAN ENTERPRISES

Create unique wall decor by decoupaging paper and adding other embellishments to a stretched canvas.

Using masking tape, mask off 11¾ x 7¾-inch rectangle on canvas, slightly above center to accommodate fringe.

Tear mulberry papers into strips; tear some small pieces from dark blue tissue. Brush decoupage medium over rectangle. Lay turquoise strips across rectangle. Brush with another layer of decoupage medium; lay on another layer of turquoise strips, then pieces of dark blue tissue. Lay white strips on top, and brush with decoupage medium. Remove tape.

Brush outer frame area with decoupage medium. Lay on larger pieces torn from dark blue tissue. Brush on more decoupage medium; lay on pieces of white mulberry paper, and light blue and dark blue tissue here and there to create different shades. Dip metallic gold thread in decoupage medium; arrange around blue frame area. Apply decoupage medium over all.

Adhere beaded trim across bottom of center rectangle using quick-setting tacky glue. Paint basswood strips black; adhere around rectangle.

Using pattern provided, cut menorah from metallic gold card stock; adhere in center of rectangle. Squeeze a pea-size drop of metallic gold dimensional paint above each candleholder in menorah; press clear stone into paint. Decorate menorah using blue dimensional paint.

Adhere blue ribbon around edges of canvas using quick-setting tacky glue.

Attach hanger to back of canvas. Or, screw eye screws into back of frame, 4 inches from ends; thread beads onto 18 inches of gold wire; wrap wire through and around eye screws, coiling ends as desired. ■

SOURCE: Decoupage medium, dimensional paints and stones from Duncan.

PATTERN ON PAGE 164

MATERIALS

16 x 12-inch artist canvas on frame
¼ x 3⁄16-inch basswood strips: 2 (11¾-inch), 2 (7¾-inch)
Tissue paper: dark blue, light blue
Textured mulberry paper: white, turquoise
Metallic gold card stock
Black acrylic paint
Dimensional paints: shiny blue, metallic gold
½-inch clear round stones
Blue beaded fringe
Individual blue beads (optional)
5⁄8-inch-wide dark blue ribbon
Metallic gold thread
Gold wire (optional)
Picture hanger or 2 small eye screws (optional)
Ruler
Brush
Matte-finish decoupage medium
Masking tape
Quick-setting tacky glue

Hanukkah Candle Wrap

DESIGN BY MARY AYRES

MATERIALS
6-inch white pillar candle
Card stock: white, light blue, blue
Plain vellum
Metallic silver ink pad
Silver webbing spray
2 silver mini brads
³⁄₈-inch-wide metallic silver ribbon
Fixative
Small sponge
¹⁄₁₆-inch circle punch
Sewing machine
Metallic silver thread
Instant-dry paper glue
Computer (optional)
Computer font (optional)

Silver webbing spray and metallic ribbon add a festive shimmer to light up the Hanukkah season.

Spray white card stock and a small piece of blue card stock with silver webbing spray; let dry. Tear 9½ x 5-inch rectangle from webbed white card stock; rub edges with silver ink using small piece of dry sponge.

Using pattern provided, cut star from light blue card stock; ink edges with silver ink pad. Adhere star to center of white webbed rectangle. Thread sewing machine with silver thread and stitch around star as indicated by dashed lines on pattern. Cut center hexagon from blue webbed card stock; ink edges with silver ink pad. Adhere hexagon to center of star.

Use computer to generate, or hand-print, "happy hanukkah" on vellum to fit within area measuring 2½ x ½ inches. Spray words with fixative. Tear vellum strip around words; lay across center of star. Punch ¹⁄₁₆-inch holes in ends of vellum; attach mini brads through holes.

Wrap white rectangle around candle, overlapping ends. Wrap ribbon around candle at top and bottom of card stock, knotting ends on back. ■

SOURCES: Webbing spray and fixative from Krylon; instant-dry paper glue from Beacon.

PATTERN ON PAGE 169

Seasonal Greetings

DESIGN BY KATHLEEN GEORGE, COURTESY OF DOW CHEMICAL CO.

Lightweight letters carved from plastic foam form the base of this dimensional wall art. Use them to decorate a wall or a door, and cover them in paper to match your favorite holiday.

MATERIALS

6-inch plastic foam letters:
    S, H, A, L, O, M
6-inch wooden dowel
Printed papers: white, blue,
    gold, silver
Acrylic paints: white pearl,
    silver, gold
11 x 42-inch strip blue fabric
Star of David sequins
Beads, rhinestones
Microglitter: white,
    silver, gold
Craft wire: silver, gold
Metallic braids, trims
Decorative cord
Craft knife
Circle punches
Hand-sewing needle and
    blue thread
Sewing machine (optional)
Iron
Paintbrush
Wire cutters
Needle-nose pliers
White craft glue

Paint individual letters silver, white pearl, or gold; paint dowel gold. Spread thin layer of glue over front of letters; sprinkle with matching microglitter. Tap glitter into the glue using your fingertips; shake off any excess glitter. Let dry.

Decorate letters with printed paper, braids and trims. *Note: For crisp, sharp edges, cut strips long so that ends overhang letters; when dry, trim ends even with edges of letters.*

Form individual squiggles and coils from wire, leaving ⅜ inch straight at each end. Bend ends down 90 degrees. Press ends into letters so that embellishments lie flush against letter.

Adhere beads, rhinestones and sequins.

Fold fabric in half, right sides facing; using sewing machine or hand-sewing needle and blue thread, seam long edges with ½-inch seam. Sew one end into a point. Clip corners at point; turn fabric inside out. Press. At top, turn under fabric and stitch to make pocket for hanging dowel. Thread dowel through pocket; tie cord around ends for hanger.

Adhere letters to fabric. ■

SOURCE: STYROFOAM® plastic foam letters from Dow Chemical Co.

Christmas Gift Pail

DESIGN BY MARY AYRES

Fill this miniature galvanized pail with favorite holiday treats. These make quick last-minute gifts for co-workers and teachers.

Sand bucket; apply one coat of sealer to all surfaces. When dry, paint all surfaces with several coats of russet paint, letting paint dry between coats, until bucket is completely covered. Brush one coat of crackle medium over sides of bucket. Let dry. Top with one coat crimson paint; cracks will appear as paint dries. Dry-brush edges of bucket with metallic gold paint.

Print Christmas images from CD-ROM onto photo paper in smallest size. **Option:** *Use stickers or images from magazines or greeting cards.* Cut out; adhere images to bucket using jewel glue. Trim edges of images that extend beyond bucket. Brush sides of bucket with one coat laminating liquid using large foam brush. Let dry. Rub fingers over any areas where paper images are coming up. Wrap jute twine around handles; adhere using permanent adhesive.

Adhere another Christmas image to tea-dyed tag; trim tag as needed. Punch $\frac{1}{16}$-inch holes through tag at corners of image; mount mini brads through photo anchors in holes. Adhere greenery to top back of tag; tie tag to handle using sisal twine. Thread red hemp cord through ornament hangers; tie in a bow around bucket handle in front of tag. ■

SOURCES: Holiday images CD-ROM from The Vintage Workshop; paints, crackle medium and sealer from DecoArt; tag from Rusty Pickle; photo anchors from Making Memories; hemp cord from Toner Plastics; decoupage medium, permanent fabric adhesive and jewel glue from Beacon.

MATERIALS

- 5¾ x 6-inch round galvanized metal bucket
- Tea-dyed tag
- Matte photo paper
- Vintage Christmas images from CD-ROM (optional)
- Acrylic paints: russet, crimson, metallic gold
- Crackle medium
- Sealer
- Laminating liquid
- 4 antique metal photo anchors
- 4 gold mini brads
- Natural jute twine
- Sisal twine
- Red hemp cord
- Christmas greenery
- Small Christmas ball ornaments
- Sandpaper
- Paintbrushes
- Large foam brush
- Paper towels
- ¹⁄₁₆-inch circle punch
- Permanent adhesive
- Jewel glue
- Computer (optional)

Paper Patchwork Stocking

DESIGN BY KATHY WEGNER

Mix and match papers for a stocking that has a whimsical quilted look. Fuzzy fibers finish off the cuff and wire coils are just for fun.

MATERIALS

Red-and-white printed
  papers
Tissue paper
Baking parchment or waxed
  paper
Flat heart buttons: 2 red,
  2 white
6 white mini spiral clips
½-inch-wide white rickrack
Fibers: 2 red, 2 white
Decorative-edge scissors
Foam brush or sponge
Hand-sewing needle
Red and white sewing
  threads
Sewing machine (optional)
Matte decoupage medium
Craft glue

Using pattern provided, trace two copies of stocking outline, reversing one, onto tissue paper. Lay patterns under baking parchment.

Cut printed papers into pieces using decorative-edge scissors. Arrange pieces over stocking patterns, overlapping edges patchwork-fashion and overlapping pattern outlines. Adhere printed papers together where they overlap using craft glue.

Coat right sides of patchwork stockings with decoupage medium using sponge; blot off excess using paper towels.

Lay patchwork shapes together, wrong sides facing; lay pattern on top. Using sewing machine or hand-sewing needle and white thread, stitch layers together over pattern lines, leaving top open. Carefully tear off pattern.

Trim straight top edge using scissors. Cut along sides and bottom using decorative-edge scissors, trimming close to stitching.

Hold four 24-inch strands of fiber together; fold in half and knot 2 inches from fold to form hanging loop. Adhere fiber tails along top edge of stocking on front and back, twisting fibers as you adhere them. Wrap extra fiber around top of stocking once more and adhere. Trim excess.

Sew thread through buttonholes, alternating colors. Adhere buttons and rickrack to both sides of stocking. Thread clips onto fibers, three on each side. ■

SOURCES: Decoupage medium from Plaid; craft glue from Beacon.

PATTERN ON PAGE 165

CD Tin

DESIGN BY LINDA BEESON

Smiling snowmen dance across the front of an altered CD tin. It's easy to change the look simply by changing the paper and embellishments.

MATERIALS

CD tin
Printed paper
Card stock
1½-inch wooden snowman cutout
Chalk ink pad
Acrylic paint
Buttons
Eyelet and eyelet-setting tool
Ribbon
Fine-grit sandpaper
Paintbrush
Hammer and nail (optional)
Circle punches: ⅛-inch, ⅝-inch
Paper glue
Craft cement

Sand tin to remove existing paint. Cut paper to fit top of lid and bottom of tin; adhere using paper glue. Paint exposed edges.

Punch two holes ¼–½ inch apart in center of lid using hammer and nail. Thread ribbon through holes in lid and large button; tie button to lid to use as handle for opening tin.

Cut tag from card stock; cover bottom portion with printed paper using paper glue. Rub edges of paper using chalk ink pad.

Punch ⅝-inch circle from printed paper; adhere to end of tag using paper glue. Punch ⅛-inch hole in end of tag, through center of paper circle; set eyelet in hole. Adhere snowman and buttons to tag using craft cement. Thread ribbon through hole in tag; tie around button on lid of CD tin. ■

SOURCES: Paper from Sweetwater; chalk ink pad from Clearsnap.

Snowman Candle

DESIGN BY SANDRA GRAHAM SMITH

Star brads attach a fun snowman motif to the front of a wintry candle wrap.

Cut 9½ x 3½-inch strip of snow words paper; wrap around center of candle, securing strip with two star brads through overlapped edges on back. Cut two 9½ x ½-inch strips of snow words paper using decorative-edge scissors; wrap around top and bottom of candle, securing each strip with a star brad through overlapped ends on back.

Stamp snowman on 1½ x 2¾-inch piece ivory card stock; stamp snowflakes all around snowman. Color snowman using colored pencils. Cut dark blue card stock 1¾ x 3 inches; cut silver card stock 2 x 3¼ inches. Center snowman on dark blue, then silver card stock. Holding layers together, punch hole in each corner of snowman rectangle, through all three layers. Insert star brads through holes; press brads through center candle strip and into candle. ■

SOURCES: Printed paper from Carolee's Creations & Co.; stamps from The Angel Company and Stampin' Up!.

MATERIALS

6-inch white pillar candle
Printed paper: snow words
Card stock: metallic silver, dark blue, ivory
Rubber stamps: snowman, snowflakes
Denim blue ink pad
Colored pencils
8 silver star brads
Decorative-edge scissors
1/16-inch circle punch

A Sweetly Scented Holiday

DESIGNS BY CRAFT MARKETING CONNECTIONS INC.

Whether you choose whimsical or traditional, you'll love using these air-freshener covers to decorate for the holidays!

NUTCRACKER

Project Note: *Adhere pieces using instant-dry paper glue unless instructed otherwise.*

Raise cone-shaped top of air freshener far enough to clear base. Wrap 1½-inch-wide strip of green/tan striped paper around base, overlapping ends on back; adhere.

Using patterns provided, cut hat from black card stock; fold on dashed line. Cut hat decoration from metallic embossed paper; adhere to hat. Adhere braid around hat, just above fold; adhere ends on back.

Using pattern provided, cut head from light tan paper; adhere hat to head. Punch hole for decorative brad through all layers using push pin; mount brad in hole. Draw facial features using blue and black markers.

Using patterns provided, cut mustache from black card stock; cut mouth from white card stock. Adhere mustache under nose. Color inside of mouth red, leaving teeth white; fold mouth and adhere fold to face.

Apply hot-glue to back of head below dotted line; adhere to front of cone, leaving 2½ inches of head protruding above cone.

Using pattern provided, cut body from red striped paper. ***Note:*** *Half of pattern is provided. Draw first half, then flip pattern along dashed line and draw other half.* Wrap body around cone, overlapping ends on back; adhere. Find center of ribbon; adhere at top edge on back of cone. Bring ends around to front; crisscrossing them as shown, and glue ends to wrong side of red striped paper at bottom. Cut prongs off all brads using craft snips; hot-glue seven mini brads down body.

Adhere three 2-inch strands of yarn down each side of head. Adhere eight 2-inch strands to face under mouth. Trim as desired.

Roll two 6 x 2¾-inch pieces red striped paper into ¾-inch-diameter tubes for arms; adhere edges. Using pattern provided, cut two epaulets from metallic embossed paper; draw ¾-inch circle in center of each on wrong side. Clip fringe from edges to center circles. Adhere epaulets over ends of arms; bend fringe down. Adhere 2½-inch piece of gold braid around open end of each arm. Hot-glue three mini brads down each sleeve. Using pattern provided, cut two hands from light tan paper; adhere hands inside arms. Adhere arms to body.

Note: *When gel is depleted, remove dried gel. From a new container, remove new, nontoxic gel; slip it over post of decorated base and reposition decorated topper. For free Renuzit Adjustable Air Freshener craft project sheets, send $1 (postage and handling) and a long, self-addressed envelope to Renuzit Crafts, CMC, 2363–460th St., Dept. HBF-Nutcracker, Ireton, IA 51027.*

MATERIALS

Adjustable cone-shaped air freshener
Card stock: black, white
Printed papers: red stripe, green/tan stripe, light tan, gold metallic embossed
½-inch decorative gold brad
13 gold mini brads
28 inches black eyelash yarn
19 inches (³⁄₈-inch-wide) dark green grosgrain ribbon
9 inches metallic gold middy braid
Permanent fine-tip markers: black, red, blue
Craft snips
Push pin
Instant-dry paper glue
Hot-glue gun and glue sticks

MATERIALS

Adjustable cone-shaped air
   freshener
Blue card stock
Swirl-printed white vellum
Mulberry paper: white, gold
Blue-and-green striped
   printed paper
3 (¾-inch) white
   snowflake brads
2 (¼-inch) round blue brads
54 inches blue/green fibers
   or ribbon
3 inches white feather boa
White acrylic paint
Black permanent fine-tip
   marker
Paintbrush
Push pin
Toothpick
Instant-dry paper glue
Permanent glue stick

SNOW FRIEND

Coat one surface of card stock using permanent glue stick. Adhere vellum to card stock. Using pattern provided, cut two snow friend body shapes from vellum-covered card stock. Punch holes for buttons and eyes in one shape using push pin.

Gently curve bodies by laying them lengthwise, and vellum side up, along table edge; with one hand on top of table, gently pull shapes around the table edge with the other hand. Mount blue brads in holes for eyes; mount snowflake brads in holes for buttons.

Run line of instant-dry paper glue along edges of one body on wrong side, beginning and ending 1½ inches from bottom; adhere second body, wrong sides facing. Let dry.

Hat: Crumple 7½ x 8-inch piece of white mulberry paper; smooth out with your fingers. Along one 7½-inch edge, fold up ½ inch twice for cuff. Wrap hat around snow friend's head, overlapping 8-inch edges on back; adhere. Adhere hat to head. Gather top of hat closed; adhere, holding until glue sets. Bend tip of hat to left; adhere. Adhere 1-inch piece cut from feather boa to tip of hat.

Cut fiber in half; tie both pieces around snow friend's neck. Referring to photo, draw facial features using black fine-tip marker. Dot highlights of white paint onto eyes using toothpick.

Nose: Fold 2 ½ x 1¼-inch piece of gold mulberry paper in half to form 1¼-inch square; roll diagonally and twist to form 1¼-inch cone; adhere to face.

Using pattern provided, cut two mittens, reversing one, from striped paper; curve over table edge, if desired. Adhere mittens to body; adhere 1-inch pieces cut of feather boa along tops of mittens. Slide snow friend over open air freshener.

Note: *When gel is depleted, replace with a new container base. For free Renuzit Adjustable Air Freshener craft project sheets, send $1 (postage and handling) and a long, self-addressed envelope to Renuzit Crafts, CMC, 236–460th St., Dept. HBF-Snowfriend, Ireton, IA 51027.* ∎

SOURCES: Renuzit LongLast Adjustable Air Fresheners from Dial Corp.; vellum from Hot Off The Press; printed papers from K&Company and Daisy D's Paper Co.; mulberry paper from The Paper Co.; instant-dry paper glue from Beacon; glue stick from 3M.

PATTERNS ON PAGE 166

"O Christmas Tree"

DESIGN BY EILEEN HULL, COURTESY OF PAPERWORK, ETC.

Punched paper snowflakes fall softly in the background of this framed Christmas tree art.

Adhere ¾-inch-wide strips of foam-core board around edges on right side of one piece of mat board. Using pattern provided, cut opening in second piece of mat board with mat cutter. ***Option:*** *Cut mat board with craft knife.* Adhere mat board to foam-core strips, right side up, on top of first mat board to create shadowbox effect.

Use computer to generate, or hand-print, "O Christmas Tree" on kraft paper to fit within 3½ x 1-inch rectangle. Cut out; trim with decorative-edge scissors. Adhere along bottom of front mat.

Adhere pewter tree plaque to black paper; cut out, leaving border. Adhere in center of cutout rectangle. Adhere glitter trees beside pewter plaque. Punch four snowflakes from kraft paper; adhere between trees and pewter plaque.

Mount picture in frame. ■

SOURCES: Plaque from Making Memories; glitter trees from EK Success; snowflake punch from Uchida of America; instant-dry paper glue from Beacon.

PATTERN ON PAGE 171

MATERIALS

2 (5 x 7-inch) pieces green
   mat board
Kraft paper
Black paper
Foam-core board
Square pewter tree plaque
2 green glitter trees
5 x 7-inch black frame
Mat cutter (optional)
³⁄₈-inch snowflake punch
Decorative-edge scissors
Instant-dry paper glue
Computer (optional)
Computer font (optional)

Holiday Sentiments

DESIGNS BY MARY AYRES

Computer-printed letters add vintage style to these unique ornaments. If you'd rather not use your computer for this project, letter stickers or rubber stamps may easily be substituted.

MATERIALS

Wooden cutouts: 3 (2-inch) squares, 4 (2⅝-inch) ovals, 3 (2-inch) circles
White card stock
Antique-style alphabet images from CD-ROM
Acrylic paints: green, light blue, pink, lavender, black, metallic gold
Iridescent ultrafine glitter
Crackle medium
Fixative
Laminating liquid
Christmas sprigs with berries
Bows of metallic ⅛-inch-wide ribbon
Metallic gold pearl cotton thread
Fine-grit sandpaper
Paintbrushes
Foam brush
Hand drill with small bit
Jewel glue
Permanent adhesive
Computer (optional)

HO HO HO

Drill holes in corners of wooden squares; sand lightly. Paint front and sides of squares black; paint crackle medium over black surfaces following manufacturer's instructions. Let dry. Paint top half of squares with one coat pink paint; paint bottom half with one coat green. Cracks will appear as paint dries. Dry-brush edges of squares with metallic gold paint.

Print "HO HO HO" from CD-ROM onto white card stock in smallest size. *Option: Stamp or hand-print letters.* Spray letters with fixative; cut out and adhere letters to squares using jewel glue, positioning H's above center and O's below. Brush laminating liquid over squares using foam brush.

Brush jewel glue over letters; sprinkle with ultrafine glitter. Remove excess glitter using a dry brush.

Thread squares onto metallic gold pearl cotton, beginning in bottom right hole and ending in bottom left hole, and leaving hanging loop at top; adhere ends on back. Adhere Christmas sprigs and ribbon bow in upper left corner of assembled ornament.

NOEL

Follow general instructions for "Ho Ho Ho," substituting wooden ovals for squares; paint two ovals green and two light blue. When threading ovals onto gold pearl cotton, run most of pearl cotton over fronts of ovals; adhere ends on back of bottom oval.

JOY

Follow general instructions for "Ho Ho Ho," substituting wooden circles for squares; paint two circles lavender and one pink. When threading circles onto gold pearl cotton, run most of pearl cotton over fronts of circles; adhere ends on back of bottom circle. ■

SOURCES: Jumbo Woodsies and drill from Forster; Antique Alphabet CD-ROM from The Vintage Workshop; paints and crackle medium from DecoArt; fixative from Krylon; decoupage medium, jewel glue and permanent fabric adhesive from Beacon.

Stackin' Snowman

DESIGN BY KATHLEEN GEORGE, COURTESY OF DOW CHEMICAL CO.

Lightweight cubes stack up to make a cute snowman with personality plus!

SNOWMAN

Cut 12½ x 3½-inch strip from embossed paper to cover sides of 3-inch cube. Fold over ½ inch along top of strip, making a sharp crease. Beginning in center of side, wrap strip around cube, crimping paper at corners; remove paper and refold sharp creases at corners.

Return paper strip to cube; adhere and pin paper in place, with bottom edges of cube and paper even. Clip corners of ½-inch excess around top; adhere and pin excess paper to top of cube. Adhere 3-inch square of embossed paper to top of cube.

Repeat to cover 4- and 5-inch cubes, using 16½ x 4½-inch and 20½ x 5½-inch strips respectively. Stack cubes and adhere to form snowman.

EMBELLISHMENTS

Adhere 6 x 1-inch strips of striped paper around dowels for arms; adhere ½-inch pompoms to one end of each. Start holes for arms in center cube using point of craft knife; add glue to holes; position arms as desired.

Wrap 12 x ¾-inch strip striped paper around neck for scarf. Gently curl two 6 x ¾-inch strips around pencil; cut ½-inch long fringe in one end of each. Glue strips to scarf off to one side.

Paint pointed end of skewer or chopstick orange; clip off. Start hole for nose in top cube using point of craft knife; add glue to hole; press nose in place.

Punch ⅜-inch circles from pink paper for cheeks; punch or cut mouth from black paper; glue cheeks, mouth and wiggly eyes to head.

Adhere strip of polka-dot paper down front of snowman; embellish with buttons. ***Option:*** *Use white paper; or substitute punched or cut paper circles for some or all of the buttons.*

Bend chenille stem into a U; adhere ends at sides of snowman's head. Adhere tinsel pompoms over ends of chenille stem. ∎

SOURCE: STYROFOAM® plastic foam cubes from Dow Chemical Co.

MATERIALS

Plastic foam cubes: 3-inch, 4-inch, 5-inch
Embossed white art paper
Printed papers: stripe, polka dot
Solid papers: pink and black, plus white, other solid colors if desired
Orange acrylic paint
2 (6-inch) dowels
Wooden skewer or chopstick
2 (½-inch), 2 (1-inch) tinsel pompoms
Chenille stem
2 wiggly eyes
Assorted small buttons (optional)
Paintbrush
⅜-inch circle punch
Pencil
Scissors
Craft knife
Craft pins
White craft glue

Twinkling Christmas Tree

DESIGN BY MARGARET HANSON MADDOX

Tiny white fairy lights adorn the front of a snowflake-covered tree. This tall tree looks great displayed in a window or on a protected porch.

MATERIALS

- 6 x 35-inch wooden tree with drilled holes on 8 x 6-inch base
- 3-inch x ¼-inch-thick wooden star
- String of 35 clear indoor twinkle lights
- 3 (12-inch) squares printed paper
- Natural handmade paper in a jar
- White acrylic paint
- Dimensional snow paint
- 20 (¾- to 1-inch) snowflake shank buttons
- White glitter
- 1-inch foam brush
- Craft knife
- Craft cutter
- Palette knife
- Transparent tape
- Tacky glue

Paint tree and star with white acrylic paint using foam brush. Tape printed paper sheets together to make a 12 x 36-inch strip; trace around tree on back of paper and cut out. Brush glue over front of tree; top with paper cutout. Poke pencil through precut holes.

Snap shanks off buttons using craft cutter; adhere to front of tree. Adhere wooden star at top. Carefully outline tree using dimensional snow paint.

Apply handmade paper to tree trunk and top of base using a palette knife; sprinkle wet paper with glitter. Let dry.

Push lights through holes in tree. ∎

SOURCES: Tree from Provo Craft; printed paper from Hot Off The Press; dimensional paint and handmade paper from DecoArt; glue from Duncan.

Simple Ornaments

DESIGNS BY NICOLE JACKSON

Sometimes less is more. Such is the case with these simple wooden ornaments that are embellished with coordinating papers and metal words.

Disassemble ornaments by untwisting wire ties and untying twine hangers. Plan which pieces you will cover with paper and which you will paint. Any pieces not covered with paper should be painted.

Using pieces of ornaments as templates, cut pieces from printed papers; adhere to front of pieces using strong cement. Repunch holes for wires and twine using needle.

Paint metal words and any pieces from ornaments that will not be covered with paper. Rub edges on ink pad as desired.

Reassemble ornaments, using new wire and twine as needed. Tie ribbon bows around twine hangers; adhere metal words to front of ornaments. ■

SOURCES: Ornaments from Provo Craft; printed papers from Melissa Frances/Heart & Home Inc., and Chatterbox; metal words from Making Memories.

Gift Tag Frame

DESIGN BY MARY AYRES

MATERIALS

- 7¾ x 8-inch flat wooden frame with 3¼-inch-square opening
- Green printed paper
- Tea-dyed tag
- Card stock: white, assorted neutral shades
- Matte photo paper
- Vintage Christmas images from CD-ROM (optional)
- 3⅜ x 1¹¹⁄₁₆-inch tag rubber stamp
- Ink pads: black, brown
- Metallic gold acrylic paint
- Black gel stain
- 2⅛ x 1⅛-inch gold bookplate
- 6 (³⁄₁₆-inch) gold eyelets and eyelet-setting tool
- 2 gold mini brads
- Hemp cord: black, red
- Sandpaper
- Paper towels
- Small sponge
- Paintbrushes
- Circle punches: ³⁄₁₆-inch, ¹⁄₁₆-inch
- ¼-inch adhesive foam squares
- Permanent adhesive
- Computer (optional)
- Computer font (optional)

Classic images of St. Nick surround a favorite family photo. Substitute nonseasonal motifs for a frame to display all year-round.

Project Note: Adhere pieces using permanent adhesive unless instructed otherwise.

Sand frame; paint with gold paint. Cut printed paper ⅜ inch smaller than frame; cut opening in center ⅜ inch larger than opening in frame. Using dry sponge, antique edges of printed paper with black ink. Center and adhere paper to frame.

Wrap black hemp cord diagonally around frame, knotting ends on front at bottom right corner and leaving long cord tails.

Stamp six tags on neutral card stock using black ink. Cut out; using dry sponge, antique edges with brown ink. Punch ³⁄₁₆-inch hole in center top of each; set eyelets in holes. Thread red hemp cord through holes; knot ends together and trim. Adhere tags to frame using adhesive foam squares, positioning tags at angles.

Print Christmas images from CD-ROM onto photo paper. *Option: Use stickers or images from magazines or greeting cards.* Cut out; adhere images to stamped tags.

Sand bookplate. Brush bookplate with black gel stain; wipe off excess using paper towel. Use computer to generate, or hand-print, "Celebrate" on white card stock to fit behind bookplate; trim card stock. On tea-dyed tag, mark positions of holes in bookplate; punch ¹⁄₁₆-inch holes through tag. Slide "Celebrate" card stock behind bookplate; mount bookplate on tag using mini brads. Trim excess tag. Thread tea-dyed tag onto ends of black hemp cord; tie in a bow. Adhere tag on top of stamped tags using adhesive foam squares. ■

SOURCES: Printed paper from K&Company; Holiday Vignettes CD-ROM from Dover Publications; tag from Rusty Pickle; rubber stamp from EK Success; hemp cord from Toner Plastics; permanent fabric adhesive from Beacon.

Christmas Roses

DESIGNS BY DIANE D. FLOWERS, COURTESY OF DOW CHEMICAL CO.

While roses aren't a traditional Christmas flower, they bring classic beauty and elegance to this trio of holiday decorations.

COLUMN

Apply hot glue to one end of a 4-inch skewer; push halfway into center of one 4-inch plastic-foam cube. Apply more hot glue to surface of cube and exposed end of skewer and press another 4-inch cube onto it to make a 4-inch-square, 8-inch-tall column.

Cut five pieces of textured wall covering to cover sides and bottom of column, centering pattern. Adhere pieces to column using glue pen. Rub on metallic gold finish to highlight texture and pattern.

Wrap two 24-inch pieces of ⅝-inch-wide red-and-gold ribbon across bottom and up sides of column, securing ends on top with floral pins. Hot-glue moss over ribbon ends to cover top of column.

Shape a 60-inch piece of ⅝-inch-wide red-and-gold ribbon into a bow with at least six loops. Secure center of bow with 6 inches of green floral wire; secure wire ends to wooden skewer with florist tape. Poke skewer into center top of column.

Apply hot glue to stems of four roses; insert one in each corner in top of column. Arrange bow loops to fill in gaps. Separate green berries into small bunches; insert them between roses and around edges on top of column.

4-INCH CUBE

Follow instructions for column, wrapping 16-inch pieces of ⅝-inch-wide red-and-gold ribbon across bottom and up sides.

5-INCH CUBE

Follow instructions for column for covering sides and bottom, wrapping 20-inch pieces of ⅝-inch-wide red-and-gold ribbon across bottom and up sides. Form bow for top from a 48-inch piece of organza ribbon; arrange 11 roses on top of cube. ■

SOURCES: STYROFOAM® brand plastic foam cubes from Dow Chemical Co.; textured wall covering from Graham & Brown; gold metallic finish from AMACO.

MATERIALS
Plastic foam cubes: 5-inch, 3 (4-inch)
Textured wall covering
19 red silk roses
6 bunches bright green berries
Green reindeer moss
Ribbon: 2½-inch-wide wire-edge red-and-gold organza, ⅝-inch-wide red-and-gold
4 (4-inch) wooden skewers
Green floral wires
Metallic gold rub-on finish
Florist pins
Shears
Green floral tape
Glue pen
Low-temperature glue gun with glue sticks

Peek-a-boo Santa

DESIGN BY LORETTA MATEIK

Combine die-cut pieces with a hand-drawn face to create a fun candy cane cover.

Referring to photo, arrange and adhere die-cut shapes together. Adhere nose and mustache using adhesive foam dots; adhere remaining pieces using glue stick.

Add details to star, hair, nose and face using fine-tip black marker. Apply pink chalk to cheeks using cotton-tip swab. Bend wire hanging loop around candy cane. Adhere assembled Santa to candy cane.

SOURCE: Die-cut shapes from Designs by Loretta.

MATERIALS

Die-cut paper shapes
Candy cane
Pink chalk
24-gauge gold wire
Black fine-tip marker
Cotton-tip swab
Adhesive foam dots
Glue stick

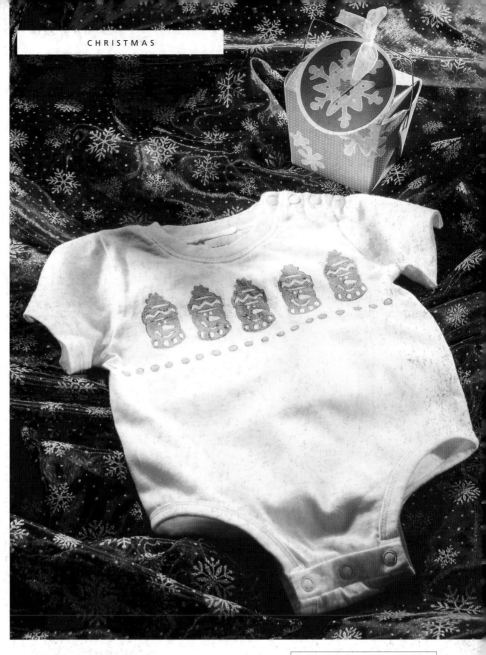

Baby's First Christmas

DESIGN BY LINDA BEESON

Craft a quick baby gift by stamping a onesie with chunky stamps and acrylic paint. Cover a Chinese take-out carton in paper with similar motifs for the coordinating gift container.

Shirt: Spread T-shirt flat. Stamp a row of snowmen across shirt using soft blue fabric paint for ink; add a row of dots underneath using round sponge applicator and soft fabric paint. Allow to dry.

Box: Take take-out container apart; spread flat. Using container as a template, cut matching shape from printed paper; stamp randomly with snowflakes using white paint as ink. Adhere paper to container using paper glue. Reassemble container.

Tag: Cut 3⅛-inch circle from blue card stock and slightly larger circle from white card stock using template cutter. **Option:** *Use patterns provided to cut circles from card stock.* Center and adhere blue circle to white one. Stamp large white snowflake in center. Personalize tag as desired. Punch ⅛-inch hole in top of tag; set eyelet in hole. Tie tag to box handle using ribbon. ■

SOURCES: Printed paper from Paper Patch; snowflake stamp and fabric paint from Duncan; template from AccuCut.

PATTERNS ON PAGE 165

MATERIALS

Chinese take-out container
Blue printed paper
Card stock: blue, white
Baby onesie T-shirt
Foam stamps: snowflakes, snowman
¼-inch round sponge applicator
Blue soft fabric paint
White acrylic paint
White eyelet and eyelet-setting tool
Sheer white ribbon
Circle template with cutter (optional)
⅛-inch circle punch
Paper glue

Westies & Scotties

DESIGNS BY HELEN L. RAFSON

Backed with formal tartan plaids, these serious pups create whimsical, holiday fun.

SCOTTY OR WESTIE

Using pattern provided, cut Scottie (facing left) from black card stock, or Westie (facing right) from white card stock. Draw dashed lines around edges using white gel pen for Scottie or black permanent marker for Westie. Dot on eye, using paintbrush handle dipped in white paint for Scottie, or black paint for Westie.

GIFT BAG

Adhere plaid paper onto side of brown paper bag, using paper glue and leaving a narrow brown paper border. Using fine-tip black marker, add dashed line around plaid paper.

Measure beaded fringe to fit across top of bag; treat ends with seam sealant and adhere fringe to bag using craft glue. Punch hearts from red card stock and plaid paper; adhere across top of fringe using craft glue.

Make Scottie or Westie; add collar and bow of red ribbon; stitch jingle bell to bow using needle and red thread. Adhere dog to plaid paper on bag using paper glue. Tie ribbon around bag handle.

PAPIER-MÂCHÉ ORNAMENT

Paint ornament with two coats red paint; let dry. Using dampened sponge, sponge ornament with gold paint; let dry. Glue metallic gold rickrack around front edge of ornament with scallops protruding past edge. Trace around ornament onto plaid paper; cut out and adhere to front of ornament using paper glue.

Make Scottie or Westie; add collar of red ribbon. Adhere dog to plaid paper on front of ornament using paper glue. Tie red ribbon in a small bow; stitch jingle bell to bow using needle and red thread. Adhere bow to ornament at top center edge.

BROWN PAPER ORNAMENT

Cut two 6-inch squares heavy brown paper; adhere them to each other using paper glue. Trim to measure 4 x 4¼ inches using decorative-edge scissors.

Center and glue 3⅝ x 3⅞-inch piece plaid paper on brown paper ornament using paper glue. Using fine-tip black marker, add dashed line around plaid paper. Punch six hearts from red card stock; adhere across top and bottom of plaid paper using paper glue.

Make Scottie or Westie; add collar of red ribbon. Adhere dog to plaid paper on front of ornament using paper glue. Form red ribbon into hanging loop with bow; stitch jingle bell to bow using needle and red thread. Adhere bow to ornament at top center edge. ∎

SOURCES: Plaid paper from Hot Off The Press; heart punch from Fiskars; paper glue and craft glue from Beacon.

PATTERN ON PAGE 168

MATERIALS

Each Project
Red/green plaid paper
Card stock: white, black
Acrylic paint: white, black
White gel pen
Black permanent fine-tip marker
¼-inch-wide red satin ribbon
9mm gold jingle bell
Paintbrushes
Hand-sewing needle and red thread
Seam sealant
Paper glue
Craft glue

Each Gift Bag
4 x 5¼-inch brown paper gift bag with handles
Red card stock
4 inches black beaded fringe
⅝-inch-wide red/green ribbon
Heart punch

Each Papier-Mâché Ornament
3⅝-inch-diameter round papier-mâché ornament
Acrylic paints: red, metallic gold
Metallic gold medium rickrack
Sponge

Each Paper Ornament
Heavy brown paper
Red card stock
Heart punch
Decorative-edge scissors

Angelic Attire

DESIGN BY MARY AYRES

Even angels need spare outfits! Create these charming miniature ornaments featuring handmade paper with added sparkle from mica chip inclusions.

MATERIALS

- 7 x 9-inch pieces card stock: pink, lavender, blue (optional), metallic white, metallic gold
- Plain vellum
- Mica dust (optional)
- Mix-ins for handmade paper: pink, lavender, blue (optional)
- Iridescent ultrafine glitter
- 3 gold mini brads
- 3 (⅛-inch) gold eyelets and eyelet-setting tool
- 22-gauge wire: pink, purple, turquoise
- 3 (4-inch) white/gold chenille stems
- Metallic gold pearl cotton thread
- Fixative
- Waxed paper (optional)
- Blender (optional)
- Pour handmold (optional)
- Iron (optional)
- Decorative-edge scissors
- Small sponge
- Circle punches: ⅛-inch, ¹⁄₁₆-inch
- Star punch
- Sewing machine
- Metallic gold sewing thread
- Jewel glue
- Permanent craft adhesive
- Computer (optional)
- Computer font (optional)

Project Note: Adhere pieces using permanent craft adhesive unless instructed otherwise.

Follow manufacturer's instructions to use pour handmold for making paper. For each sheet, tear one color of pastel card stock—pink, lavender or blue—into pieces; place in blender with ¼ teaspoon mica dust and several matching mix-ins (no pods). Place handmade paper between sheets of waxed paper; iron until dry. *Option: Use ready-made handmade paper or mulberry paper.*

Using patterns provided, cut wings from metallic white card stock and gown from pink, lavender or blue handmade paper; trim bottom edges of wings and gown using decorative-edge scissors.

Thread sewing machine with metallic gold thread; machine-stitch around gown ⅛ inch from edge. Punch star from metallic gold card stock; adhere to gown. Punch ¹⁄₁₆-inch hole through star; set mini brad in hole. Dab jewel glue along bottom edges of wings and gown using dry sponge; sprinkle with ultrafine glitter.

Using pattern provided, form hanger from matching wire. Adhere gown to wings, sandwiching hanger in between.

For tag, use computer to generate, or hand-print, Christmas message on vellum to fit within an area approximately 1½ x ¾ inches. Spray with fixative. Tear vellum around words, leaving room at left end for eyelet. Punch ⅛-inch hole in tag; set eyelet in hole. Tie tag to hanger with metallic gold pearl cotton. Adhere tag to right side of gown and wings.

For halo, bend chenille stem into an oval with ends in the center. Hang halo on hanger; adhere, positioning ends behind hanger. Knot hanging loop of gold pearl cotton over hanger hook. ■

SOURCES: Papermill Pour Handmold, mica dust and Angel Wings paper additives from Arnold Grummer's; wire from Toner Plastics; fixative from Krylon; star punch from EK Success; jewel glue and permanent fabric adhesive from Beacon.

PATTERNS ON PAGE 170

Christmas Tree Centerpiece

DESIGN BY SUSAN STRINGFELLOW

Vibrant lime green and cherry red papers cover plastic foam balls to create a lively holiday tree.

MATERIALS
9-inch plastic foam cone
11 or 12 (2-inch) plastic
    foam balls
Black metal pillar
    candle stand
Christmas printed papers
White tissue paper
Gold leaf
Metal leaf adhesive size
Ribbons: red, green, gold
Rickrack
Gloss varnish
Paintbrushes
Soft toothbrush
Toothpicks
Wooden chopstick
⅝-inch circle punch
Decoupage medium
Glue

Paint candle stand with metal leaf adhesive; let dry. Press gold leaf sheets onto candle stand; brush off excess using a soft toothbrush. Coat stand with varnish.

Adhere plastic foam cone to base using glue. For each plastic foam ball, cut a 3 x 6¼-inch strip printed paper; fringe long edges on both sides, making 1¼-inch-long cuts every ¼ inch. Adhere fringed paper strips around balls using decoupage medium and overlapping fringe strips to cover ball. Punch ⅝-inch circles from contrasting paper; adhere to balls where ends of fringes meet. Using toothpicks, anchor balls to tree.

Coat exposed areas of cone with decoupage medium. Press 3-inch squares of white tissue into wet decoupage medium using chopstick.

Fold 6- or 7-inch lengths of ribbons and rickrack into thirds so that you have a loop and ribbon end sticking out. Press ribbon and rickrack loops into wet decoupage medium on cone using chopstick. ∎

SOURCES: STYROFOAM® plastic foam cone and balls from Dow Chemical Co.; printed papers from Daisy D's Paper Co.; gold leaf and metal leaf adhesive size from Mona Lisa Products; decoupage medium from Plaid.

Holiday Glow Frame & Lamp

DESIGNS BY BARBARA GREVE

MATERIALS
- Small candle-bulb lamp with shade
- 6½ x 5-inch flat wooden frame
- 4 used dryer sheets
- White tissue paper
- White vellum
- Acrylic paints: cranberry, red, teal, green
- White chalk
- Fabric lace sticker
- 2 crystal marquise-shaped "jewels"
- Metal snowflake charm
- Black alphabet rub-on transfers
- Metallic gold 4-ply thread
- ½-inch-wide sheer metallic gold ribbon
- Pressing paper
- Iron
- Spray bottle with water
- Small sponge
- Stapler
- Vellum tape
- Fusible web
- Permanent adhesive

An interesting technique using tissue paper and dryer sheets creates a very textured surface. Choose colors of acrylic paint to make a set that matches your decor.

Project Note: Adhere all pieces using permanent adhesive unless instructed otherwise.

PAPER

Heat iron to low setting used for synthetic fabrics; press dryer sheets to remove wrinkles. Lay 27 x 12-inch piece pressing paper on ironing board shiny side up; lay dryer sheets on top, side by side. Lay a 25 x 9-inch piece fusible web over dryer sheets, edges even. Swirl metallic gold thread all over fusible web in overlapping loops and curves.

Crinkle tissue paper; tear it into strips and lay the over the fusible web, leaving gaps between the strips so that metallic thread will show through here and there. Cover all layers with another piece of pressing paper, shiny side down, and fuse according to manufacturer's instructions; let cool.

Thin each color of paint in a separate container to the consistency of skim milk. Spritz fused layers with water, then sponge a different color over each area that is covered with crinkled tissue. Spritz again with water to allow paint to bleed out into open areas. Keep varying and blending colors until all the crinkled tissue sections are stained. Let dry.

LAMP SHADE

Lay shade on its side on paper; mark where bottom and top edges touch paper using white chalk. Roll lamp shade over paper, continuing to mark paper at top and bottom of shade, until starting point is reached. Cut out the lamp-shade pattern, cutting ³⁄₁₆ inch outside chalked lines to allow extra for folding over. Fit paper over lamp shade, folding edges over top and bottom, and overlapping ends. Adhere paper to shade along top, bottom and where paper overlaps on ends.

FRAME

Trace and cut paper to fit on front of frame; adhere. Transfer "joy" to center of a 2¾ x ⅞-inch strip of vellum; adhere vellum to center of fabric lace sticker using vellum tape. Adhere jewels over ends of lace sticker; adhere lace sticker across center bottom of frame. Thread ribbon and gold thread through hole in snowflake charm; staple fibers together just above charm. Adhere charm to upper right area of frame. ■

SOURCES: Paints from DecoArt; sticker from EK Success; alphabet transfers and snowflake charm from Making Memories; permanent fabric adhesive from Beacon.

Victorian Gift Cones

DESIGN BY MARY AYRES

Fill these special ornaments with tiny gifts and treats. They also double as stylish tree ornaments.

Using pencil, trace cutting lines from template onto front of desired card stock. Randomly stamp gold images all over traced shape. Cut out cone; transfer fold lines to back of shape.

Cut metallic gold paper to line each petal at top of cone; adhere to backs of petals. Punch ⅛-inch hole on opposite sides of cone, positioning holes 1 inch below top fold. Set eyelets in holes.

Assemble cone. Thread ends of a 12-inch piece of ribbon through eyelets; knot ends inside cone. Fill box with treats or gift; fold petals to close cone. Embellish cone as desired, adding a pink ribbon bow. ∎

SOURCES: Cone template from Duncan; rubber stamps from Delta/Rubber Stampede and Anna Griffin; permanent fabric adhesive from Beacon.

MATERIALS

Petal-top cone template
Card stock: white, ivory, light green
Metallic gold paper
Rubber stamps
Pencil
Metallic gold ink pad
6 (⅛-inch) gold eyelets and eyelet-setting tool
¼-inch-wide pink satin ribbon
Desired embellishments: brass charms, buttons, lace, greenery, etc.
⅛-inch circle punch
Permanent craft adhesive

Christmas Tree Gift Set

DESIGNS BY MARY AYRES

Buttons and wool felt add dimension to this quick-and-easy coordinating candle and gift-card set.

MATERIALS

6-inch ivory pillar candle
Red card stock
Green wool felt
2 gold eyelets and eyelet-
    setting tool
Flat buttons: 3 (½-inch),
    3 (⅝-inch)
Cinnamon sticks
⅛-inch-wide wire-edge
    metallic gold ribbon
Ivory pearl cotton or
    embroidery floss
Texturizing plate
Embossing tool
³⁄₁₆-inch circle punch
Sewing machine
Metallic gold sewing thread
Embroidery needle
Rotary cutting tool with
    scoring blade (optional)
Permanent adhesive

CANDLE

Using patterns provided, cut candle tag from red card stock and candle tree from wool felt. Emboss vertical lines on tag using texturizing plate and embossing tool. Thread sewing machine with metallic gold thread; machine-stitch around tag ⅛ inch from edge. Punch ³⁄₁₆-inch hole in top of tag; set eyelet in hole.

Adhere felt tree to tag. Using embroidery needle, poke holes through tree and tag as shown by dots on pattern. Stitching through holes, work blanket stitch around edge of felt tree using embroidery needle and one strand ivory pearl cotton (or three plies separated from a strand of embroidery floss); adhere knots on back.

Thread needle with several strands of metallic gold thread; stitch thread through buttons, knotting ends on front. Adhere buttons to tree using permanent adhesive; adhere 1-inch piece of cinnamon stick to tag for tree trunk.

Position center of ribbon on back of tree near top; bring ends around candle and through eyelet in tag from back to front; take ribbons down and around to back of candle; knot ends tightly. Wrap a second piece of ribbon around candle, tying ends in a bow over cinnamon stick. Secure ribbons with permanent adhesive.

CARD

Referring to instructions for candle and using patterns provided for card, cut tag-shaped card from folded red card stock, positioning dashed line on fold. Emboss front of card and machine-stitch around edges. Add tree and eyelet to front of card, using ⅝-inch buttons and a 1½-inch piece of cinnamon stick. Glue bow of gold ribbon to front of card over tree trunk. ■

SOURCES: Embossing tool from Fiskars; permanent fabric adhesive from Beacon.

PATTERNS ON PAGE 168

Silent & Soft & Slow descends the SNOW
-Henry Wadsworth Longfellow

Sparkle Candle Shade

DESIGN BY SANDRA GRAHAM SMITH

Pierced paper allows the warm glow of a tea light to shine through this sparkling snowflake candle shade.

Using pattern provided, cut candle shade from card stock. Trim top edge using decorative-edge scissors; punch 1/16-inch holes as desired to enhance pattern.

Stamp snow saying in center of shade. Stamp snowflakes around saying and over rest of shade.

Lay stamped shade facedown on light box. **Option:** *Tape shade in a sunny window, wrong side facing you.* Lightly trace around stamped snow words and larger snowflakes on wrong side of shade with a pencil. Lay shade facedown on plastic foam sheet or other work surface; use pin to poke evenly spaced holes on penciled lines around stamped images.

Turn shade right side up. Embellish larger stamped snowflakes with glitter glue; adhere page pebbles over smaller stamped snowflakes.

Adhere ends of candle shade using tacky craft glue and overlapping ends about ½ inch. Adhere a strip of double-sided adhesive inside shade around bottom edge; peel off backing and adhere beaded fringe to adhesive strip.

Place tea light candle in goblet; top goblet with shade. **Note:** Never *leave burning candle unattended.* ∎

SOURCES: Rubber stamps from Duncan, Hero Arts, Inkadinkado and Delta/Rubber Stampede; page pebbles from Making Memories; beaded fringe from Decorative Details.

PATTERN ON PAGE 169

MATERIALS

- Ivory stardust card stock
- 10¾-ounce wine goblet
- Tea light candle
- Rubber stamps: snow saying, snowflakes
- Denim blue ink pad
- Glitter glue
- 3/8-inch clear round page pebbles
- Clear/pearl beaded fringe
- Decorative-edge scissors
- 1/8-inch circle punch
- Straight pin
- Light box (optional)
- Plastic foam sheet or other flat work surface
- Tacky craft glue
- Double-sided adhesive strips

Collage Ornaments

DESIGNS BY SANDRA GRAHAM SMITH

Use one basic pattern to create a variety of charming gift tags that also double as tree ornaments.

MATERIALS
Each Tag
Thick cardboard
Metallic silver marker
Colored pencils
Eyelet-setting tool
Decorative-edge scissors
Glue stick
⅛-inch circle punch
"Believe"
Printed paper: red, green
Card stock: dark green,
    black, ivory, red
Vellum saying
Santa rubber stamp
Black ink pad
Black embroidery floss
5 red (5mm) buttons
⅛-inch red eyelet
Punches: small tree, holly
Winter Wonderland
Printed papers: blue, dark
    blue
Sparkle paper
Card stock: ivory, blue
Snowman rubber stamp
Denim blue ink pad
Liquid glitter
White/silver embroidery floss
⅛-silver silver eyelet
1-inch snowflake punch

"BELIEVE"

Using pattern provided, trace and cut tag from cardboard. Trace and cut two tag shapes from red printed paper; glue one to back of cardboard tag. Set tag aside.

Trace outline of tag top onto green printed paper; cut out, tearing across bottom edge; adhere across top quarter of remaining red paper tag. Trace and cut second green print to fit in lower right corner; adhere to red paper tag.

Stamp Santa onto ivory card stock; color with colored pencils. Cut out using decorative-edge scissors; adhere to red card stock. Cut out using decorative-edge scissors, leaving narrow border; adhere to black card stock. Cut out using regular scissors, leaving narrow border; adhere Santa to red/green paper tag.

Tear around vellum saying; adhere to front of paper tag using two red buttons. Punch one tree and three holly leaves from dark green card stock; adhere holly leaves in upper right corner and tree at bottom left. Attach three red buttons over leaves for holly berries. Adhere entire decorated red/green panel to front of cardboard tag.

Punch hole in top of tag; set eyelet in hole. Thread embroidery floss through hole for hanging loop. Color edges of tag using silver marker.

WINTER WONDERLAND

Using pattern provided, trace and cut tag from cardboard. Trace and cut two tag shapes from blue printed paper; glue one to each side of cardboard tag.

Cut dark blue paper strip to fit across tag; trim long edges using decorative-edge scissors. Adhere paper to tag; trim ends. Embellish design on blue printed paper using liquid glitter.

Stamp snowman onto ivory card stock; color with colored pencils. Cut out; adhere to dark blue card stock. Cut out, leaving narrow border; adhere to sparkle paper. Cut out, leaving narrow border; adhere snowman to tag. Punch two snowflakes from sparkle paper; adhere to tag.

Punch hole in top of tag; set eyelet in hole. Thread embroidery floss through hole for hanging loop. Color edges of tag using silver marker. ■

SOURCES: Printed papers from Bo-Bunny Press, Carolee's Creations & Co. and American Traditional Designs; vellum saying from The C-Thru Ruler Co.; rubber stamps from Duncan and Stampin' Up!.

PATTERN ON PAGE 171

CD Gift Folder

DESIGN BY LINDA BEESON

MATERIALS
Card stock CD folder
Printed papers: green, red
Black card stock
Black label-tape stickers
Rub-on transfers: black and
    white letters and numerals
Black bookplate
Red heart-shape eyelet and
    eyelet-setting tool
2 black mini brads
Green acrylic paint
Red button
Ribbon
Sewing needle and red
    thread
Paintbrush
Paper piercer or awl
⅛-inch circle punch
Paper glue

Tuck a photo CD in a custom-made holder that also includes a pocket to hold a personalized message or card.

Carefully undo glued edges and open CD folder; spread flat. Paint inside green. Cover inside folders with red printed paper; embellish with label stickers. Cover exterior of folder with green printed paper.

Punch two small holes ½ inch apart in right-hand edge of folder using paper piercer; thread 6-inch piece of ribbon through holes and knot ends on outside to make loop for closing folder.

Punch holes through front cover near right-hand edge, opposite ribbon loop. Stitch button to cover through holes using needle and red thread.

Punch two more holes through spine of folder, near top and about ½ inch apart. Thread both ends of a 10-inch piece of ribbon through top hole from outside to inside, and back out through bottom hole; knot ends to form hanging loop.

Cut black card stock to fit behind bookplate. Transfer title to card stock using white rub-on transfers. On front cover, mark positions of holes in bookplate; punch ⅛-inch holes through cover. Slide title behind bookplate; mount bookplate on cover using mini brads. Transfer year, other words, etc., to folder using rub-on transfers.

Refold folder; adhere using paper glue. To close, wrap ribbon on right edge around button on cover. ■

SOURCES: CD folder from River City Rubber Works; printed papers from Sweetwater and Provo Craft; label stickers from K&Company; bookplate from Li'l Davis Designs; rub-on transfers from Making Memories.

Holiday Seasonings

DESIGN BY SHERRY WRIGHT

After you've altered every other surface imaginable, try your salt and pepper shakers to spice up your holiday meals.

Paint shaker lids red using foam brush, keeping holes open.

Coat glass surfaces of shakers with decoupage medium; immediately cover with black toile tissue. Let dry overnight.

Apply decoupage medium to top half of shakers; immediately wrap 1-inch-wide strips of green printed paper around shakers over decoupage medium. Apply decoupage medium to bottom half of shakers; immediately wrap with 1-inch-wide strips of red printed paper. Let dry overnight.

Lightly sand painted tops and corners of shakers for a distressed look.

Tie a 22-inch piece of ribbon in a bow around each shaker; adhere using adhesive dots. Adhere bottle-cap stickers to bottle caps; adhere bottle caps near bottom of shakers using adhesive dots. ■

SOURCES: Anchor Hocking salt and pepper shakers; printed papers from Creative Imaginations; printed tissue from DMD Inc.; bottle caps and stickers from Design Originals; decoupage medium from Plaid.

MATERIALS

Glass salt and pepper shakers
Black toile printed tissue
Printed papers: red, green
Red acrylic paint
2 bottle caps
2 Christmas bottle-cap stickers
3/8-inch-wide black-and-white gingham ribbon
Paintbrush
Foam brush
Sandpaper
Decoupage medium
Adhesive dots

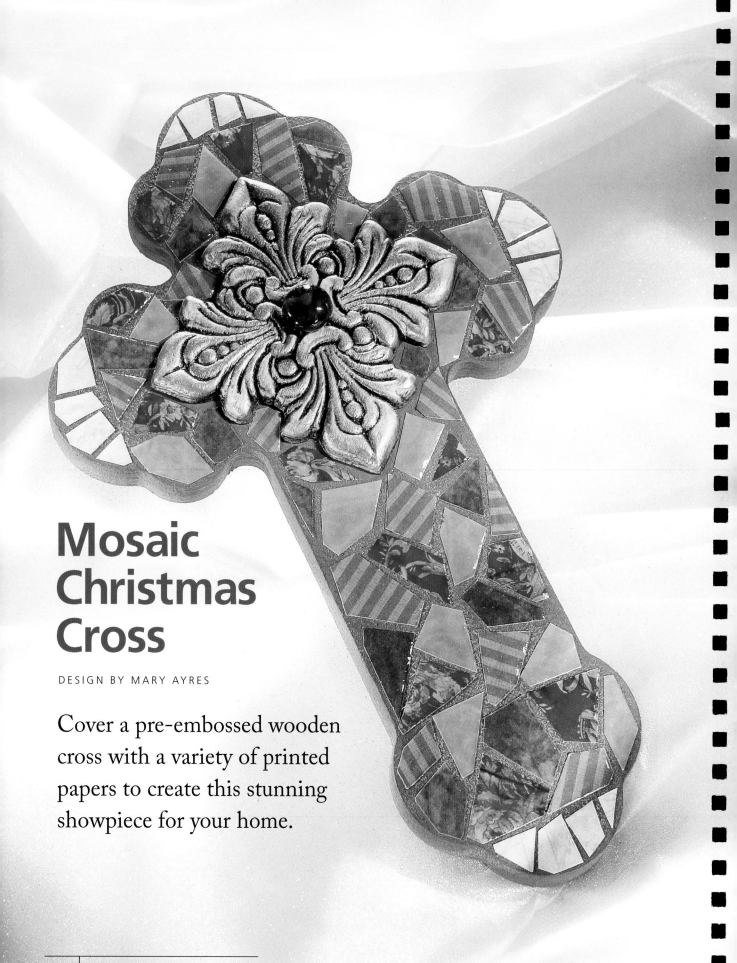

Mosaic Christmas Cross

DESIGN BY MARY AYRES

Cover a pre-embossed wooden cross with a variety of printed papers to create this stunning showpiece for your home.

Lightly sand cross. Paint embossed detail gold; let dry. Brush black gel stain on embossed detail; using dampened paper towel, quickly wipe off excess, leaving color in crevices. Dry-brush embossed detail with cream paint.

Paint flat surfaces of cross light brown. Mix equal parts light brown paint and texturizing medium. Dab mixture onto front and sides of cross, avoiding embossed detail, to give cross a textured appearance. Let dry. Dry-brush edges of cross with dark brown paint.

Cut tiles in random shapes from printed papers. Beginning at ends with light tiles and working toward center with medium to dark ones, position tiles on cross, leaving space between them. Using paper glue, adhere tiles to cross. Paint a single heavy coat of paper glaze over each tile. Let dry overnight. Apply a second coat of paper glaze; let dry overnight.

Adhere red marble in center of embossed detail using craft cement. Attach hanger to back of cross. ■

SOURCES: Cross from Walnut Hollow; printed papers from K&Company; texturizing medium and gel stain from DecoArt; paper glaze from Duncan.

MATERIALS

7 x 11-inch flat wooden cross with embossed detail

Printed papers with "texture" patterns: 1 light, 4 medium to dark

Acrylic paints: cream, light brown, dark brown, metallic gold

Black gel stain

Texturizing medium

Paper glaze

Flat-back translucent red marble

Fine-grit sandpaper

Bristle paintbrushes

Paper towels

Hanger with mounting hardware

Paper glue

Craft cement

MATERIALS

Mat board: green, red, off-white
Corrugated cardboard
Tan card stock
6¼ x 3⅛-inch red tags
Christmas postal rubber stamps
Alphabet rubber stamps
Ink pads: green, red
2 silver eyelets and eyelet-setting tool
2 silver star snaps
Silver bookplate
1-inch silver wire hoop
Beads
"Enjoy" zipper pull
Fibers
⅛-inch circle punch
Double-sided tape
Computer (optional)
Computer font (optional)

Merry Christmas Tag Book

DESIGN BY EILEEN HULL, COURTESY OF PAPERWORK, ETC.

Keep your various Christmas lists together in one book. Fill the pages of this tag book with lists of holiday gift and card recipients, as well as photos and memories.

Cut two pieces green mat board 6½ x 3½ inches for covers; stamp with Christmas postal images using green ink pad. Center and punch a ⅛-inch hole near left edge on each cover; set eyelets in holes.

Cut 3½ x 1-inch strip red mat board. Use computer to generate, or hand-print, "christmas" on tan card stock to fit behind bookplate. Mark positions of bookplate holes on red mat board strip; punch ⅛-inch holes through mat board. Slide title behind bookplate; mount bookplate on red mat board using star snaps. Adhere red mat board to front cover near bottom.

Cut five ¾-inch squares from off-white mat board and five 1-inch squares from corrugated cardboard. Stamp letters for "merry" on mat board squares using red ink pad; center and adhere a letter on each corrugated square. Adhere corrugated squares to cover.

Decorate tags as desired for pages. Add computer-generated or hand-printed lists, gift ideas, holiday poems, etc.; decorate with Christmas snapshots, rub-ons, printed paper accents, stickers, etc.

Thread covers and pages on wire hoop; add zipper pull, beads and fibers to hoop. ∎

SOURCE: Rubber stamps from Hero Arts.

Bottle-Cap Ornaments

DESIGNS BY SUSAN STRINGFELLOW

These fun ornaments feature a retro look and the option of finishing them as shakers. The jingle bells add a little bit of extra pizzazz!

"JOY"

Project Note: *Adhere all pieces using paper glaze.*

Flatten bottle caps using rubber mallet. Punch two holes in each bottle cap near edges on opposite sides using hammer and nail. Punch or cut six 1¹⁄₁₆-inch circles from printed paper; adhere to both sides of bottle caps.

Use computer to generate, or hand-print, letters to spell "JOY" on transparency. ***Option:*** *Use rub-on transfers.* Punch circles from transparency with letters in centers.

Sprinkle clear fine glitter into bottle caps so that they will act as shakers. With holes at top and bottom, adhere transparency letters over glitter in bottle caps, applying a thin line of paper glaze around edges.

String bottle caps together using 2½-inch pieces pink rickrack. In bottom hole, attach jingle bell using 2½-inch piece sheer green ribbon. In top hole, tie another 2½-inch piece sheer green ribbon, and add a hanging loop of fine gold cord.

"NOEL"

Project Note: *Adhere all pieces using paper glaze.*

Flatten bottle caps using rubber mallet. Punch two holes in each bottle cap near edges on opposite sides using hammer and nail. Adhere bottle-cap stickers on back of each bottle cap; rub edges with caramel ink.

Punch or cut four 1¹⁄₁₆-inch circles from printed paper; adhere to front (concave) sides of bottle caps.

Use computer to generate, or hand-print, letters to spell "NOEL" *reversed* on back of black card stock; cut out using craft knife. ***Option:*** *Use rub-on transfers.* Adhere a letter to front of each bottle cap. Apply a layer of paper glaze over letters.

String bottle caps together using 2½-inch pieces of ribbon. In bottom hole, attach jingle bell using another 2½-inch piece of ribbon. In top hole, tie a hanging loop of fine gold cord. ■

SOURCES: Bottle caps and stickers from Design Originals; printed paper from DieCuts With A View and KI Memories; paper glaze from JudiKins.

MATERIALS

3 bottle caps
Pink/green printed papers
Printable transparency
Clear fine glitter
Gold jingle bell
⅝-inch-wide sheer green ribbon
Pink rickrack
Fine gold cord
Rubber mallet
Hammer and small nail
1¹⁄₁₆-inch circle punch
Large-eye needle
Paper glaze
Computer (optional)
Computer font (optional)

MATERIALS

4 bottle caps
4 holiday bottle-cap stickers
Holiday printed papers
Black card stock
Caramel ink
Gold jingle bell
⅜-inch-wide red/green ribbons
Fine gold cord
Rubber mallet
Hammer and small nail
1¹⁄₁₆-inch circle punch
Craft knife
Large-eye needle
Paper glaze
Computer (optional)
Computer font (optional)

Moments to Remember

CONTINUED FROM PAGE 12

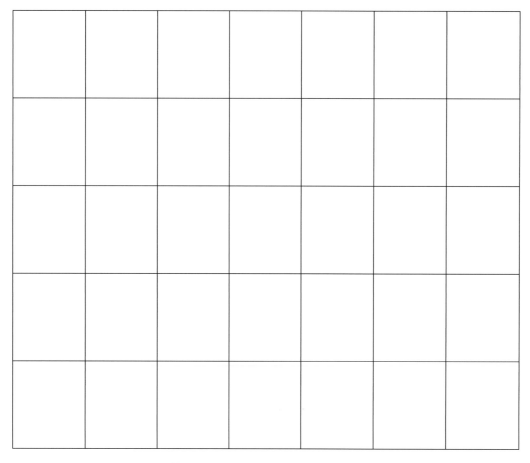

Moments to Remember Calendar Page

Floral Fantasy Party Set

CONTINUED FROM PAGE 15

STEMWARE COLLARS

Following instructions for larger flowers, make larger single-layer flowers from card stock. Using craft knife, cut ½-inch opening in center, large enough to admit stem of glass. Cut straight from outer edge to center opening; slide collar around stem of glass. ■

SOURCES: STYROFOAM® brand plastic foam cube from Dow Chemical Co.; rubber stamps from Outlines Rubber Stamp Co. and Magenta; paper glue from Beacon.

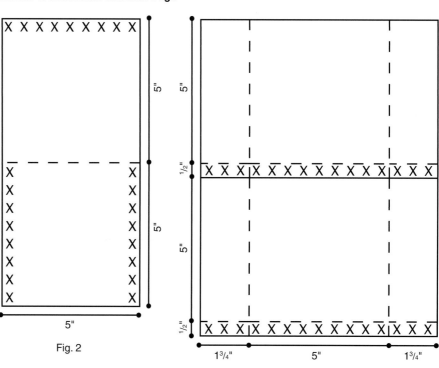

Fig. 2

Fig. 1

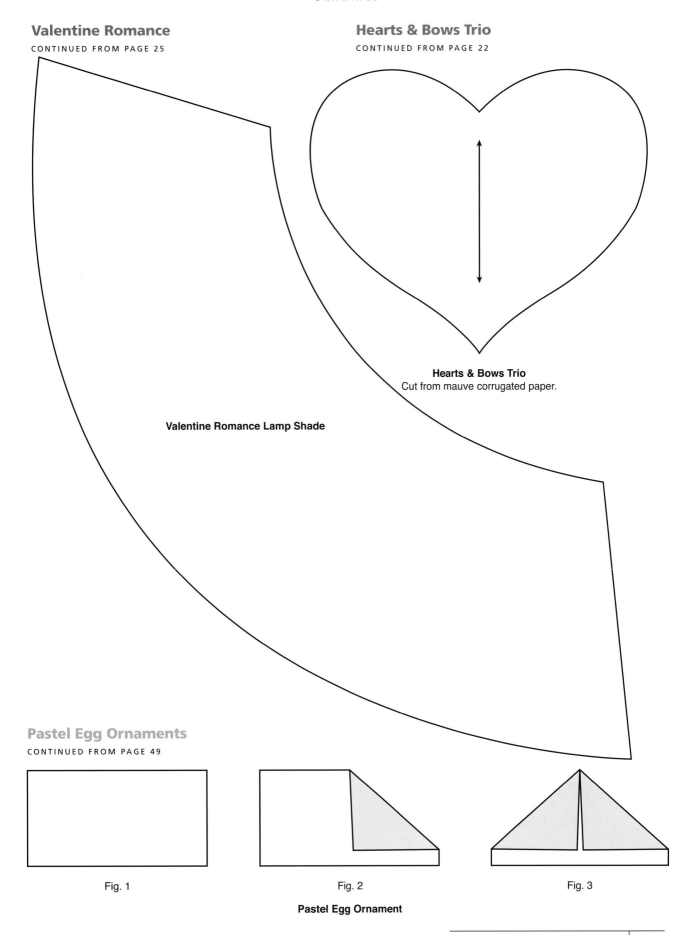

Valentine Romance
CONTINUED FROM PAGE 25

Hearts & Bows Trio
CONTINUED FROM PAGE 22

Hearts & Bows Trio
Cut from mauve corrugated paper.

Valentine Romance Lamp Shade

Pastel Egg Ornaments
CONTINUED FROM PAGE 49

Fig. 1

Fig. 2

Fig. 3

Pastel Egg Ornament

Bunny Notes

CONTINUED FROM PAGE 51

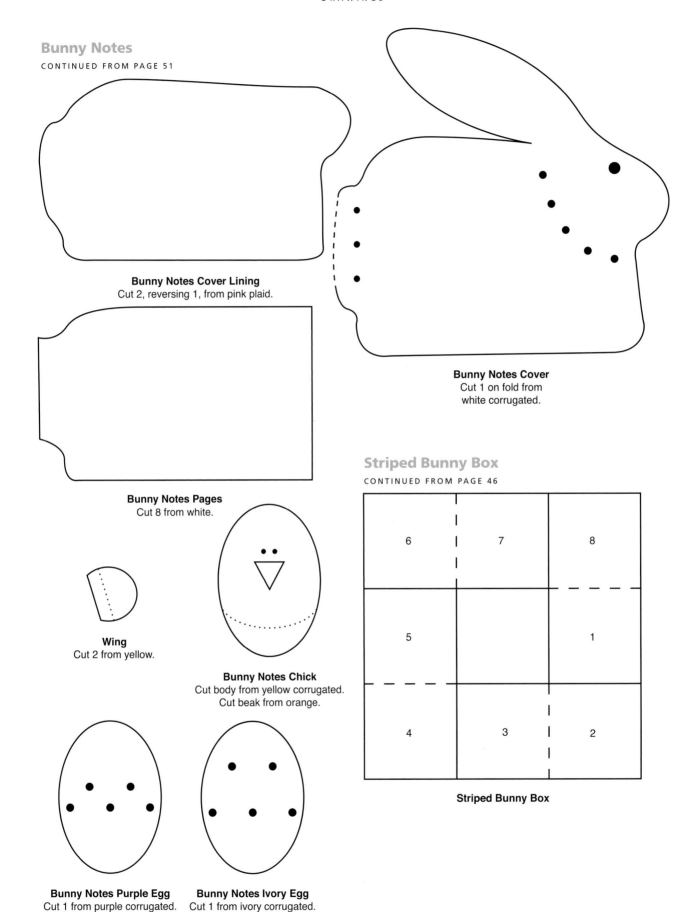

Bunny Notes Cover Lining
Cut 2, reversing 1, from pink plaid.

Bunny Notes Cover
Cut 1 on fold from
white corrugated.

Bunny Notes Pages
Cut 8 from white.

Wing
Cut 2 from yellow.

Bunny Notes Chick
Cut body from yellow corrugated.
Cut beak from orange.

Bunny Notes Purple Egg
Cut 1 from purple corrugated.

Bunny Notes Ivory Egg
Cut 1 from ivory corrugated.

Striped Bunny Box

CONTINUED FROM PAGE 46

6	7	8
5		1
4	3	2

Striped Bunny Box

Bunny Tic-Tac-Toe
CONTINUED FROM PAGE 52

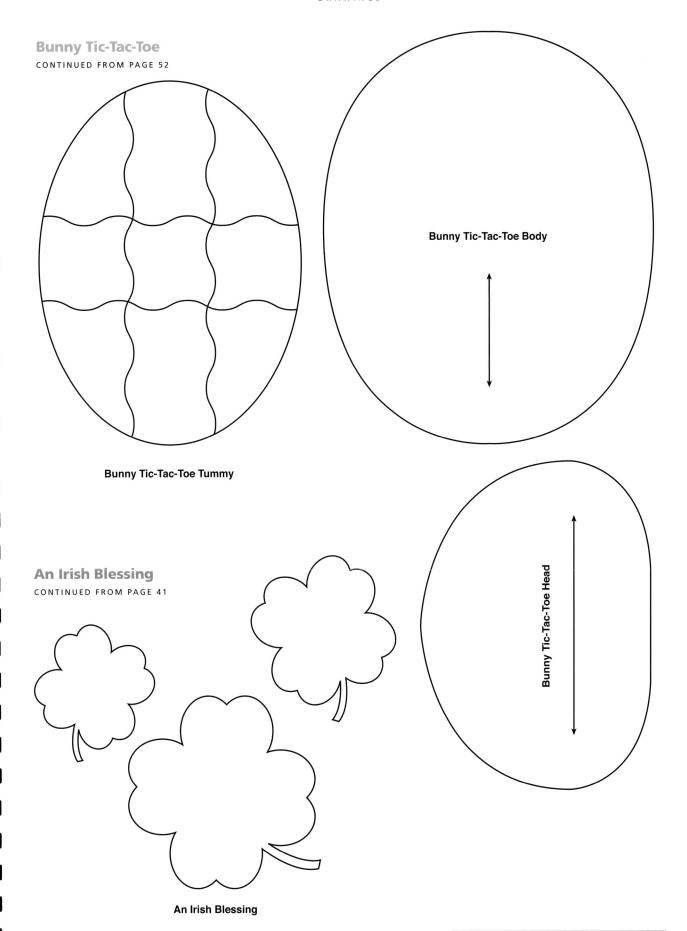

Bunny Tic-Tac-Toe Body

Bunny Tic-Tac-Toe Tummy

Bunny Tic-Tac-Toe Head

An Irish Blessing
CONTINUED FROM PAGE 41

An Irish Blessing

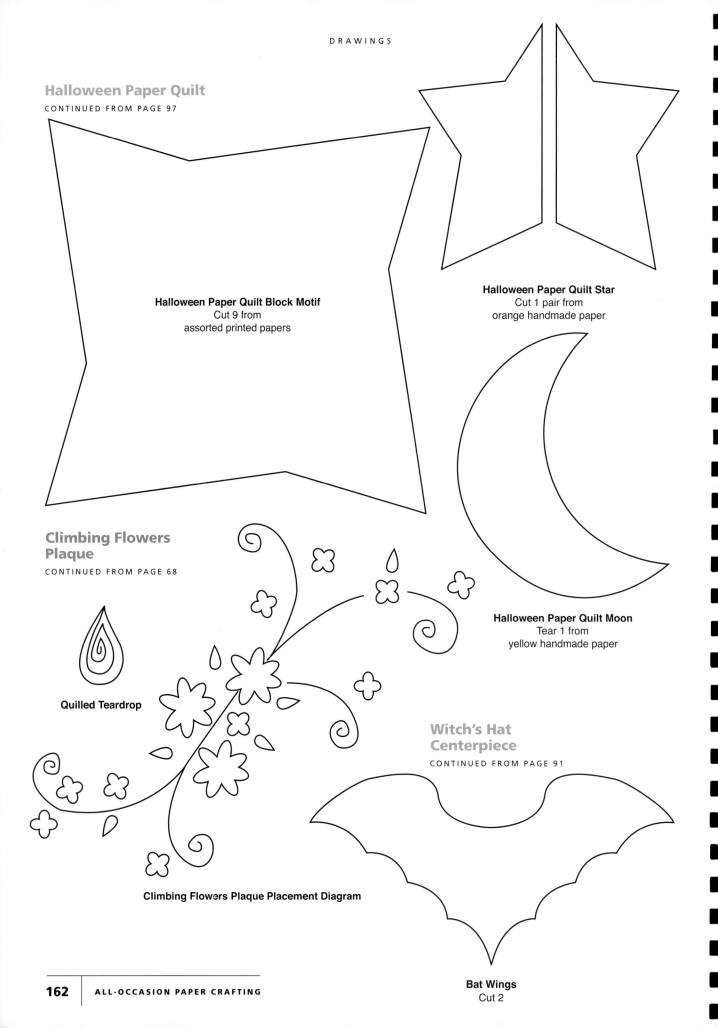

Halloween Paper Quilt
CONTINUED FROM PAGE 97

Halloween Paper Quilt Block Motif
Cut 9 from
assorted printed papers

Halloween Paper Quilt Star
Cut 1 pair from
orange handmade paper

Halloween Paper Quilt Moon
Tear 1 from
yellow handmade paper

Climbing Flowers Plaque
CONTINUED FROM PAGE 68

Quilled Teardrop

Climbing Flowers Plaque Placement Diagram

Witch's Hat Centerpiece
CONTINUED FROM PAGE 91

Bat Wings
Cut 2

Easter Take-Out
CONTINUED FROM PAGE 43

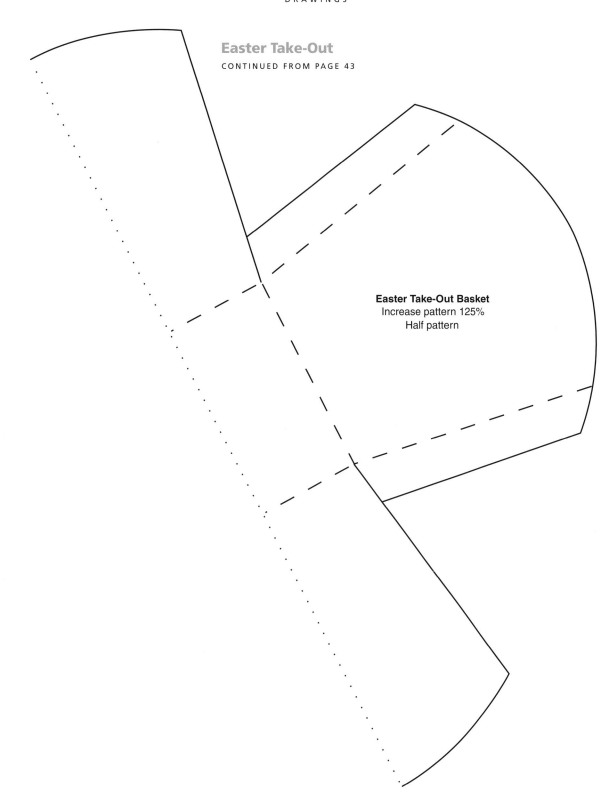

Easter Take-Out Basket
Increase pattern 125%
Half pattern

Hanukkah Wall Canvas
CONTINUED FROM PAGE 111

Hanukkah Wall Canvas
Cut 1 from gold card stock

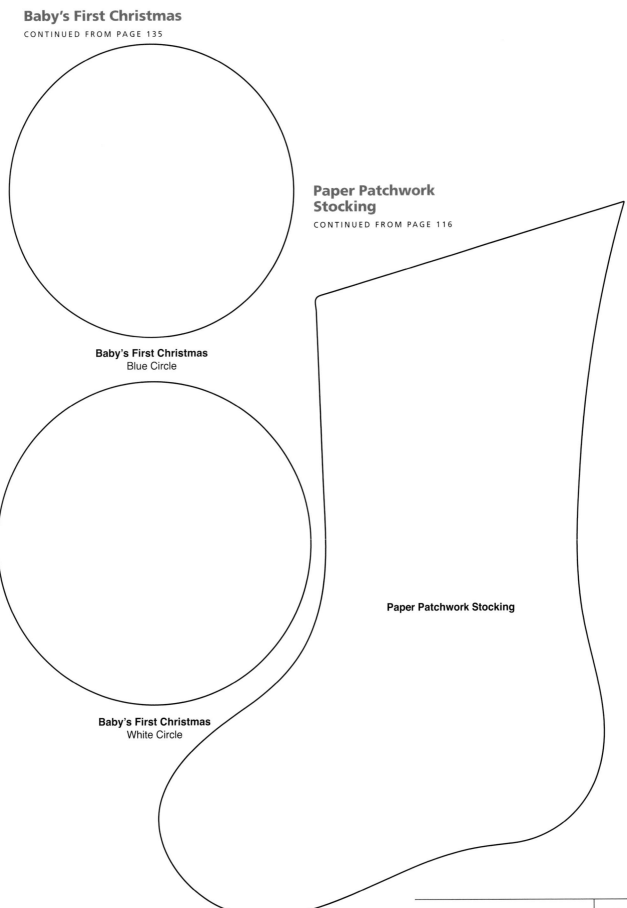

Baby's First Christmas
CONTINUED FROM PAGE 135

Baby's First Christmas
Blue Circle

Paper Patchwork Stocking
CONTINUED FROM PAGE 116

Paper Patchwork Stocking

Baby's First Christmas
White Circle

A Sweetly Scented Holiday

CONTINUED FROM PAGE 122

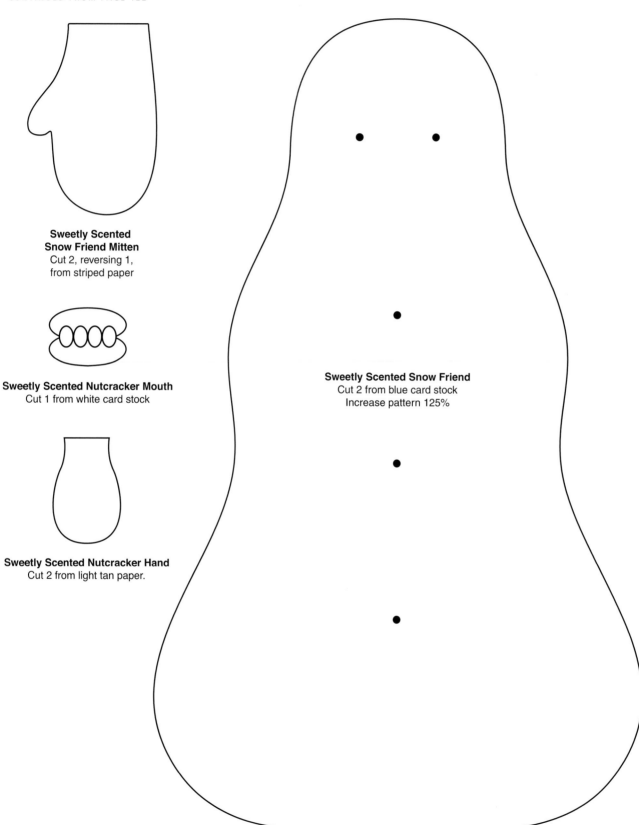

**Sweetly Scented
Snow Friend Mitten**
Cut 2, reversing 1,
from striped paper

Sweetly Scented Nutcracker Mouth
Cut 1 from white card stock

Sweetly Scented Nutcracker Hand
Cut 2 from light tan paper.

Sweetly Scented Snow Friend
Cut 2 from blue card stock
Increase pattern 125%

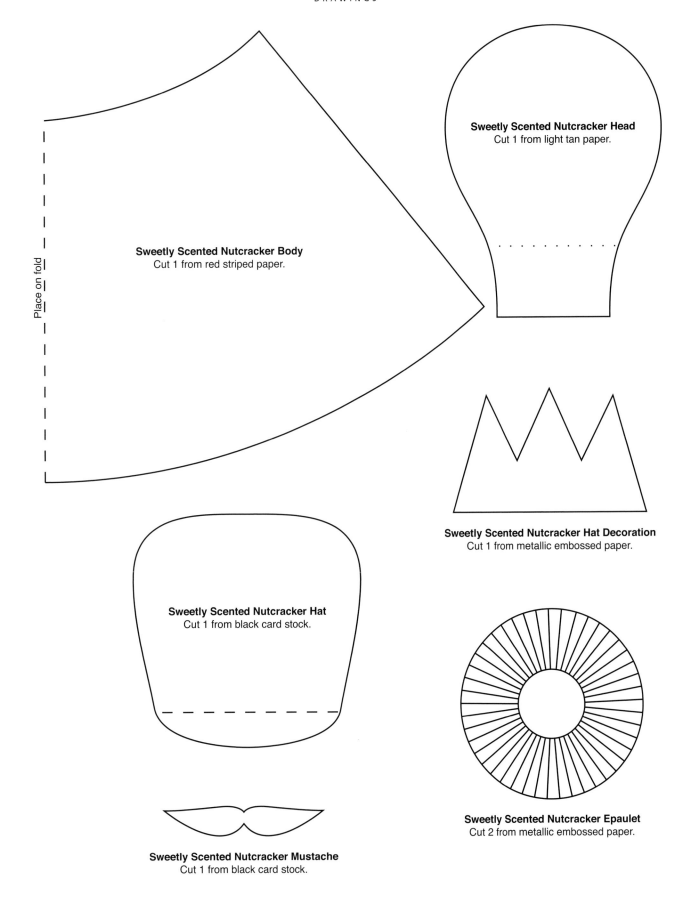

Sweetly Scented Nutcracker Body
Cut 1 from red striped paper.

Place on fold

Sweetly Scented Nutcracker Head
Cut 1 from light tan paper.

Sweetly Scented Nutcracker Hat Decoration
Cut 1 from metallic embossed paper.

Sweetly Scented Nutcracker Hat
Cut 1 from black card stock.

Sweetly Scented Nutcracker Epaulet
Cut 2 from metallic embossed paper.

Sweetly Scented Nutcracker Mustache
Cut 1 from black card stock.

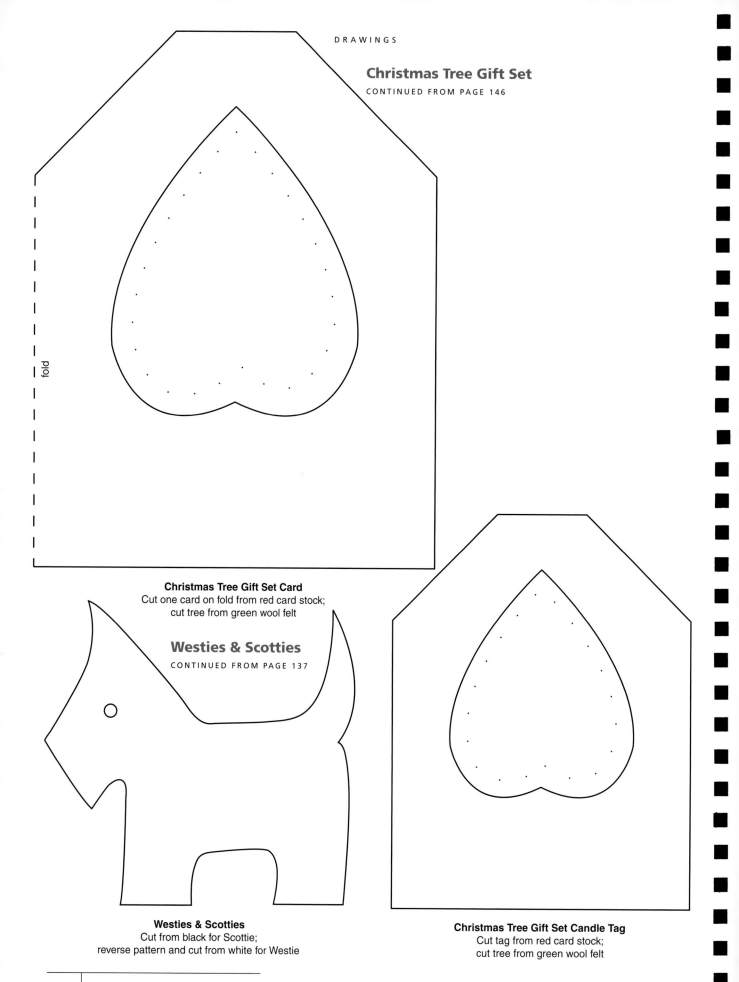

Christmas Tree Gift Set

CONTINUED FROM PAGE 146

fold

Christmas Tree Gift Set Card
Cut one card on fold from red card stock;
cut tree from green wool felt

Westies & Scotties

CONTINUED FROM PAGE 137

Westies & Scotties
Cut from black for Scottie;
reverse pattern and cut from white for Westie

Christmas Tree Gift Set Candle Tag
Cut tag from red card stock;
cut tree from green wool felt

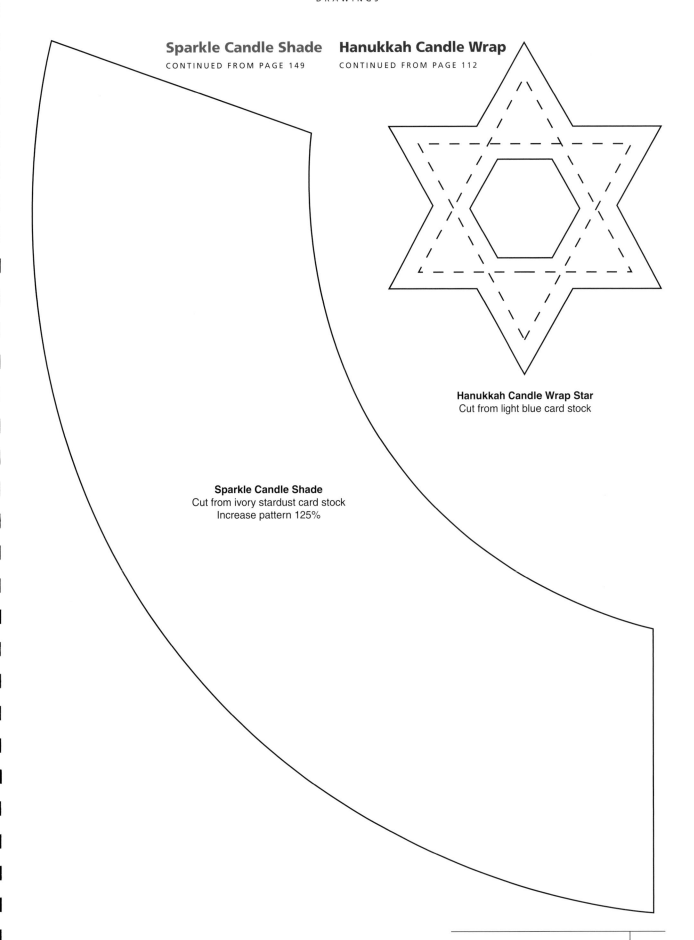

Sparkle Candle Shade
CONTINUED FROM PAGE 149

Hanukkah Candle Wrap
CONTINUED FROM PAGE 112

Hanukkah Candle Wrap Star
Cut from light blue card stock

Sparkle Candle Shade
Cut from ivory stardust card stock
Increase pattern 125%

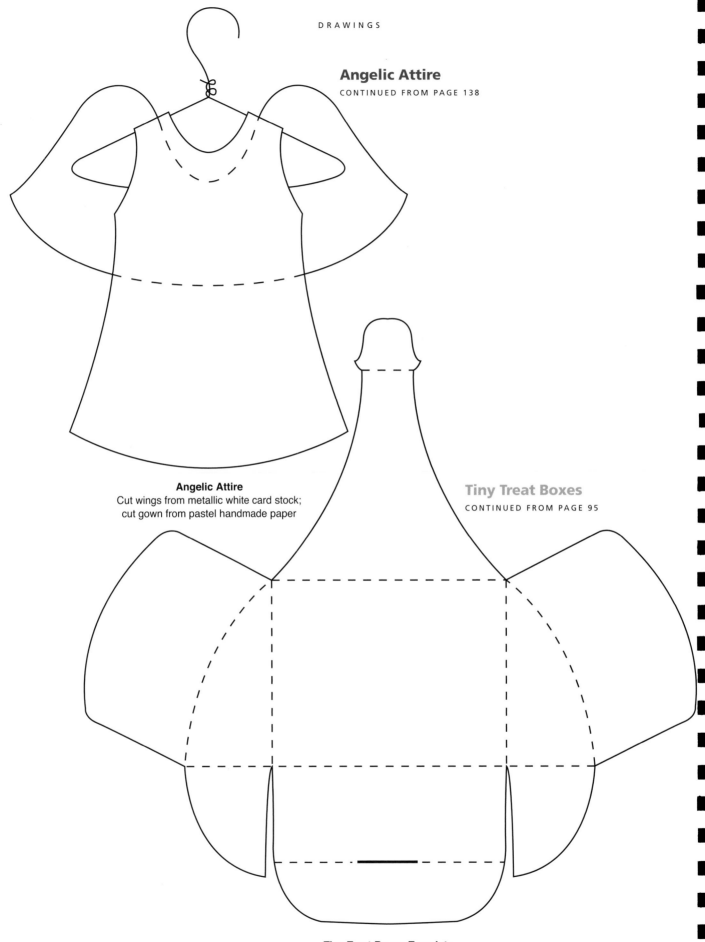

Angelic Attire
CONTINUED FROM PAGE 138

Angelic Attire
Cut wings from metallic white card stock;
cut gown from pastel handmade paper

Tiny Treat Boxes
CONTINUED FROM PAGE 95

Tiny Treat Boxes Template

"O Christmas Tree"
CONTINUED FROM PAGE 123

"O Christmas Tree" Mat
Cut 1 from green mat board

Collage Ornaments
CONTINUED FROM PAGE 150

Collage Ornaments Tag
Cut 1 from cardboard for each ornament
cut 2 from red paper for "Believe";
cut 2 from blue paper for Winter Wonderland

General Instructions
Paper crafting is easy, creative and fun. Collect basic tools and supplies, learn a few simple terms and techniques, and you're ready to start. The possibilities abound!

Cutting & Tearing

Craft knife, cutting mat Must-have tools. Mat protects work surface, keeps blades from getting dull.

Measure and mark Diagrams show solid lines for cutting, dotted lines for folding.

Other cutters Guillotine and rotary-blade paper cutters, oval and circle cutters, cutters that cut unusual shapes via a gear or cam system, swivel-blade knives that cut along the channels of plastic templates, and die-cutting machines (large or small in size and price). Markers that draw as they cut.

Punches Available in hundreds of shapes and sizes ranging from $1/16$ inch to over 3 inches (use for eyelets, lettering, dimensional punch art, and embellishments). Also punches for two-ring, three-ring, coil, comb and disk binding.

Scissors Long and short blades that cut straight or a pattern. Scissors with nonstick coating are ideal for cutting adhesive sheets and tape, bonsai scissors best for cutting rubber or heavy board. Consider comfort—large holes for fingers, soft grips.

Tearing Tear paper for collage, special effects, layering on cards, scrapbook pages and more. Wet a small paintbrush; tear along the wet line for a deckle edge.

Embellishments

If you are not already a pack rat, it is time to start! Embellish projects with stickers, eyelets, brads, nail heads, wire, beads, iron-on ribbon and braid, memorabilia and printed ephemera.

Embossing

Dry embossing Use a light source, stencil, card stock and stylus tool. Add color, or leave raised areas plain.

Heat embossing Use embossing powder, ink, card stock and a heat tool to create raised designs and textures.

Powders come in a wide range of colors. Fine grain is called "detail" and heavier is called "ultrathick." Embossing powders will not stick to most dye inks—use pigment inks or special clear embossing inks for best results.

Glues & Adhesives

Basics Each glue or adhesive is formulated for a particular use and specified surfaces. Read the label and carefully follow directions, especially those that involve personal safety and health.

Foam tape adds dimension.

Glue dots, adhesive sheets and cartridge type machines quick grab, no drying time needed.

Glue pens Fine line control.

Glue sticks Wide coverage.

Repositionable products Useful for stencils and temporary holding.

Measuring

Rulers A metal straightedge for cutting with a craft knife (a must-have tool). Match the length of the ruler to the project (shorter rulers are easier to use when working on smaller projects).

Quilter's grid ruler Use to measure squares and rectangles.

Pens & Markers

Choose inks (permanent, watercolor, metallic, etc.), **colors** (sold by sets or individually), **and nibs** (fine point, calligraphy, etc.) **to suit the project.** For journals and scrapbooks, make sure inks are permanent and fade-resistant.

Store pens and markers flat unless the manufacturer says otherwise.

Scoring & Folding

Folding Mountain folds—up, valley folds—down. Most patterns will have different types of dotted lines to denote mountain or valley folds.

Tools Scoring tool and bone folder. Fingernails will scar the surface of the paper.

Paper & Card Stock

Card stock Heavier and stiffer than paper. A sturdy surface for cards, boxes, ornaments.

Paper Lighter-weight surfaces used for drawing, stamping, collage.

Storage and organization Store paper flat and away from moisture.

Arrange by color, size or type. Keep your scraps for collage projects.

Types Handmade, milled, marbled, mulberry, origami, embossed, glossy, matte, botanical inclusions, vellum, parchment, preprinted, tissue and more.

Stamping

Direct-to-paper (DTP) Use ink pad, sponge or stylus tool to apply ink instead of a rubber stamp.

Inks Available in pads and re-inker bottles. Types include dye and pigment, permanent, waterproof and fade-resistant or archival, chalk finish, fast drying, slow drying, rainbow and more. Read the labels to determine what is best for a project or surface.

Make stamps Carve rubber, erasers, carving blocks, vegetables. Heat Magic Stamp foam blocks to press against textures. Stamp found objects such as leaves and flowers, keys and coins, etc.

Stamps Sold mounted on wood, acrylic or foam, or unmounted (rubber part only), made from vulcanized rubber, acrylic or foam.

Store Flat and away from light and heat.

Techniques Tap the ink onto the stamp (using the pad as the applicator) or tap the stamp onto the ink pad. Stamp with even hand pressure (no rocking) for best results. For very large stamps, apply ink with a brayer. Color the surface of a stamp with watercolor markers (several colors), huff with breath to keep the colors moist, then stamp; or lightly spray with water mist before stamping for a very different effect.

Unmounted stamps Mount temporarily on acrylic blocks with Scotch Poster Tape on one surface (nothing on the rubber stamp) or one of the other methods (hook and loop, paint on adhesives, cling plastic).

Buyer's Guide

Projects in this book were made using products provided by the manufacturers listed below. Look for the suggested products in your local craft- and art-supply stores. If unavailable, contact suppliers below. Some may be able to sell products directly to you; others may be able to refer you to retail sources.

3M
www.3m.com

7gypsies
(877) 749-7797
www.sevengypsies.com

Accucut
(800) 288-1670
www.accucut.com

Adhesive Products Inc.
(510) 526-7616
www.crafterspick.com

Altered Pages
(405) 360-1185
www.alteredpages.com

AMACO/American Art Clay Co. Inc.
(317) 244-6871
www.amaco.com

American Traditional Designs
(800) 448-6656
www.americantraditional.com

Amscan
(800) 335-7585
www.amscan.com

The Angel Co.
(785) 820-9181
www.theangelcompany.net

Anna Griffin Inc.
(404) 817-8170
www.annagriffin.com

Arnold Grummer's
(800) 453-1485
www.arnoldgrummer.com

Autumn Leaves
(800) 453-1485
www.autumnleaves.com

Basic Grey
(801) 544-1116
www.basicgrey.com

Bazzill Basics Paper
(480) 558-8557
www.bazzillbasics.com

Beacon Adhesives Inc.
(914) 699-3400
www.beaconcreates.com

Bo-Bunny Press
www.bobunny.com

Candle Magic
(304) 269-6558
www.candlemagic.com

Carolee's Creations & Co.
(435) 563-1100
www.carolees.com

Chatterbox
(888) 416-6260
www.chatterboxinc.com

Clearsnap Inc.
(888) 448-4862
www.clearsnap.com

Close to My Heart
www.closetomyheart.com

Colorbök
(734) 424-0505
www.colorbok.com

Craft Catalog
(800) 777-1442
www.craftcatalog.com

Creative Candleworks
(239) 463-9863

Creative Imaginations
(714) 500-1200
www.cigift.com

Creative Impressions
(719) 596-4860
www.creativeimpressions.com

Creative Paperclay Co. Inc.
(805) 484-6648
www.paperclay.com

C-Thru Ruler Co.
(800) 243-8419
www.cthrurulercom.com

Daisy D's Paper Co.
(888) 601-8955
www.daisydspaper.com

Darice Inc.
mail-order source: **Bolek's**
(330) 364-8878

DecoArt
(606) 365-3193
www.decoart.com

Decorator's Solution
(800) 261-4772
www.decoratorssolution.com

Delta/RubberStampede
(800) 423-4135
www.RubberStampede.com

Design Originals
(800) 877-7820
www.d-originals.com

Designs by Loretta
www.designsbyloretta.com

Destination Stickers & Stamps Inc.
(866) 806-7826
www.destinationstickers.com

The Dial Corp.
(877) 736-8148
www.dialcorp.com

Die Cuts With A View
(801) 224-6766
www.diecutswithaview.com

DMD Industries Inc./ Paperbilities
(800) 805-9890
www.dmdind.com

Doodlebug Design Inc.
(801) 966-9952
www.doodlebug.ws

Dover Publications
www.doverpublications.com

Dow Chemical Co.
Customer Information Center:
(800) 441-4369
www.dow.com

Duncan Enterprises
(800) 438-6226
www.duncancrafts.com

EK Success Ltd.
(800) 524-1349
www.eksuccess.com

Ellison
(800) 253-2238
www.ellison.com

Fibers By The Yard
(405) 364-8066
www.fibersbytheyard.com

Fiskars Brands Inc.
(866) 348-5661
www.fiskars.com

Flair Designs
(888) 546-9990
www.flairdesignsinc.com

Forster/Jarden Home Products
www.alltrista.com

Imagination Project Inc./ Gin-X
(888) 477-6532
www.imaginationproject.com

Graham & Brown
(800) 328-8452
www.grahambrown.com

Halcraft USA
(212) 376-1580
www.halcraft.com

Heidi Grace Designs Inc.
(866) 89-HEIDI
www.heidigrace.com

Hero Arts Rubber Stamps
(510) 652-6055
www.heroarts.com

Hirschberg Schutz
(908) 810-111

Hot Off the Press
(888) 300-3406
www.hotp.com

Inkadinkado
(800) 523-8452
www.inkadinkadoo.com

Jacquard Products: Rupert, Gibbon & Spider Inc.,
(800) 442-0455
www.jacquardproducts.com

Jest Charming Embellishments
(702) 564-5101
www.jestcharming.com

JudiKins
(310) 515-1115
www.judikins.com

Junkitz
(732) 792-1108
www.junkitz.com

K&Company
(816) 389-4150
www.kandcompany.com

Karen Foster Design
www.scrapbookpaper.com

Keeping Memories Alive
(800) 419-4949
www.keepingmemoriesalive.com

KI Memories
(972) 243-5595
www.kimemories.com

Kopp Design
(801) 226-1262
www.koppdesign.com

Krylon/Sherwin-Williams Co.
Craft Customer Service:
(800) 4KRYLON
www.krylon.com

LazerLetterz
www.lazerletterz.com

Li'l Davis Designs
(949) 838-0344
www.lildavisdesigns.com

The Little Scrapbook Store
(864) 228-6432
www.thelittlescrapbookstore.com

Magenta
(450) 922-5253
www.magentastyle.com

Magic Scraps
(972) 238-1838
www.magicscraps.com

Magnetic Poetry
(800) 370-7697
www.magneticpoetry.com

Making Memories
(801) 294-0430
www.makingmemories.com

MaVinci's Reliquary
www.crafts.dm.net/mall/reliquary

May Arts
(203) 637-8366
www.mayarts.com

me & my BIG ideas
(949) 583-2065
www.meandmybigideas.com

Melissa Frances/Heart & Home Inc.
(905) 686-9031
www.melissafrances.com

Mona Lisa Products– Houston Art Inc.
(717) 462-1086
www.houstonart.com

NRN Designs
(714) 898-6363
www.nrndesigns.com

Outlines Rubber Stamp Co. Inc.
(860) 228-3686
www.outlinesrubberstamp.com

Designer Index

Project Index